Handbook

for

Christian Writers

Handbook

for

Christian Writers

compiled by
Christian Writers Institute

Creation House
Carol Stream, Illinois

Sixth edition
© 1974 by Creation House. All rights reserved.
Published by Creation House, 499 Gundersen Drive,
Carol Stream, Illinois 60187.
In Canada: Beacon Distributing Ltd.,
104 Consumers Drive, Whitby, Ontario L1N 5T3

Printed in the United States of America
by George Banta Co.

International Standard Book Number 0-88419-074-9
Library of Congress Catalog Card Number 73-92316

Contents

Preface

Grace Livingston Hill is recognized as one of the most successful novelists writing on the Christian theme. Whenever she sat down to the typewriter to compose a novel she could be virtually assured that it would become a best seller.

In her halycon days, the early part of the 20th century, a starry-eyed admirer once accosted her after a public appearance. "Your stories are so wonderful! How do you get the inspiration for them?"

With a chuckle the matronly-appearing author remarked wryly, "I simply get out my checkbook. If the balance is low I start writing."

Actually, the advice is not as materialistic as it may appear. This is attested to by the fact that Miss Hill, whose books are often ridiculed for their plots by more urbane writers, knew her market so well that today something of a Grace Livingston Hill revival is underway and her better books are available in paperback on the newsstands.

The point is, the secret to becoming a successful writer—in Grace Livingston Hill's day or now—is not to climb some ivied ivory tower and brood over paper and typewriter until you finally emerge with a fistful of clean, crisp manuscript pages. Unless you begin at the marketplace your chances for success in selling a book or magazine manuscript are slim indeed.

This is the reason for the handbook for writers—and specifically this 6th edition. Here you will find a complete listing of all markets for religious or inspirational manuscript material, complete with specifications as to the requirements of the publishers or producers with proper names and addresses.

In addition you will find helpful articles by editors and publishers to whom you will be submitting your manuscripts. Their suggestions may prove to be your pathway to print and your key to a successful writing career, helping provide the helpful, inspirational material so desperately needed in our day.

Now, perhaps more than at any time in world history, men are discovering that the answer to their desires for peace, prosperity, and understanding of their fellowmen, depends first upon their recognition of the mighty hand of God in the affairs of mankind. And as a print communicator you can be the catalyst to open men's eyes to their need for committing themselves to Jesus, God's Son, whom the Bible describes as "the way, the truth and the life."

ROBERT WALKER

EDITOR, *CHRISTIAN LIFE*

PRESIDENT, CHRISTIAN WRITERS INSTITUTE

Part One
You Have an Idea

1
On Getting Article Ideas

David R. Enlow
Director of Communications,
Medical Assistance Programs, Inc.

Sanctified imagination probably will be your greatest asset in looking for article ideas. But there are other practical ways of cultivating the kind of curiosity that will keep you continuously supplied with more ideas than you know what to do with.

Many new writers, in particular, immediately think of organizations when faced with the task of discovering a possible article subject. Why not do an article on Pioneer Girls, or Child Evangelism Fellowship, or Campus Crusade for Christ? Potentially, all of these are interesting, readable subjects. But the writer must ask himself or herself several important questions before pursuing them: What market will be interested in the subject? Has it been covered recently? Is there some current, up-to-date development in the organization that lends significance to this new coverage?

After all, most Christians already know about these organizations. Ideally, a query letter is the best way to insure an editor's interest in your idea. Only if you are reasonably sure the subject will be acceptable for a certain publication should you proceed without the query letter. Be specific in your query. Don't say, "I'm going to Nepal for a week. Would you like to see an article on my trip?" Say, "I'm going to Nepal. While there I'll have a chance to interview a man, _____name_____ , who's been in prison for 10 years because he's a Christian. Would you be interested in an article about him?" This is where thinking through your general idea comes in.

An invaluable way to accumulate article ideas is to keep a notebook, preferably small enough to carry with you at all times. Jot down every hunch, every tip, every bonafide idea that comes to mind. Review your list regularly, so that you might look for additional material on each subject.

Remember, there are very few completely new ideas—and that should be good news for all aspiring writers. No extensive research or travel is required to come up with marketable ideas. Many articles are based on the calendar: Fourth of July, Washington's Birthday, etc. Others are seasonal: football, baseball, house painting, gardening, etc.

Close observation, which comes from such invaluable training as newspaper reporting, is an important way to garner ideas. Here are two personal examples to illustrate.

One day I overheard someone tell how a local physician had replied to a question about his health by remarking, "I had a good time being sick." After several interviews with the doctor, I "ghosted" the article for him, and it appeared in April 1973 *Christian Life* under the title, "I Had a Good Time Being Sick."

On vacation one year, I heard an unusual sermon on tithing—unusual in that a Baptist pastor was speaking against tithing. A question and answer interview followed, which is now in the hands of an editor.

These are only suggestive, but they may help to whet your appetite to keep eyes and ears open at all times. Article ideas are everywhere.

2
Does David C. Cook Want This?

Isabel Erickson
Editor, New Products Department,
David C. Cook Publishing Co.

The David C. Cook Publishing Company is looking for book-length manuscripts that will interest, inform, educate, and entertain children, young people, and adults in the church as well as on the street.

If you have an idea for a book, ask yourself the following questions:

1. Is your idea contemporary? Is your material factually up-to-date?

2. Is your subject of importance in the lives of people you know?

3. Do you write from a well-informed, well-researched point of view?

4. Does your treatment go deeper than the surface, studying underlying causes and positive ideas for action?

13

5. Is your subject of wide enough interest outside your group (age level, locale, income level, etc.)?

6. If there are other books on this subject already published, would yours be sufficiently unique to warrant publication?

7. Do you write to the average reading level, informing and not writing down?

8. Do you intermingle personal illustration and concrete examples with philosophical perspective, generalization and topical consideration?

9. Do you limit your scope sufficiently so that covering the topic is not an impossible task?

10. Does the subject warrant book-length treatment or could it be sufficiently explored in an article?

11. Is it distinctively Christian—is Christ honored through the content and perspective of the book?

The range of topics available to you is endless. Most of the best books begin with personal experience. What special areas of life are you involved in? What perspective can you offer as a Christian, and what light can you shed on the topic itself, the history of the problem or issue and a constructive solution, conclusion, or summation?

Consider such topics as the many aspects of education: child welfare, evangelism, special education and training of the handicapped, adult education, home Bible training, the teaching of values, physical education and the Christian, and many more.

Or Christian service possibilities: What unique ministry have you been involved in or informed about? What new areas of service are opening up on a large scale?

Or biography: What interesting people or person do you know (of); have you researched about? Do you feel strongly that his (their) story should be told?

Or personal experience: What unusual story do you have to tell about your history, life, personal battle(s), conversion experience, etc.?

Or historical fiction: write as though you were there.

Or issues: What carefully researched information can you offer on a topic of current interest such as race relations, war, missions, literacy, poverty, health, economics, communications?

Or marriage and the family: There is a demand for Christian books offering help and commentary in the important area of family relationships.

As you narrow down your chosen topic, ask yourself again the above 11 questions.

Manuscripts should be around 40,000 words in length, typed doublespaced, 50 characters per line. Submit an original typed copy, not a photocopy. Keep a copy of the manuscript yourself—don't let go of your only copy.

Submit a query letter to find out the editor's interest in your topic. If the reply is favorable, you will probably be asked to submit an outline of the way you intend to develop your book, plus a sample chapter.

Address queries to:

> Mrs. Isabel Erickson, Editor
> New Products Department
> David C. Cook Publishing Co.

3
Is It for Campus Life?

Harold Myra
Editor, Campus Life

Writing for the youth market in *Campus Life* may not be easy for everyone, but it can be rewarding.

As in almost all writing for magazines, the first rule is to study in-depth the particular publication. We feel very strongly about this at *Campus Life.* In the choice of material and the slanting of material we have a certain thing we're looking for, and to find out what that is you need to study the magazine. Getting a full year's worth of the magazine and becoming immersed in the material is the best way to get a feel for what we need. And if this seems to be a bit too much research, then probably you should not write for *Campus Life.*

While we're being negative, we'll throw in one more item. Youth is a mind set, and if you just normally plug into it, then it may be a natural for you to write for young people. But if in order to write for young people—to get a message across to these kids who need it—you need deep research and don't really understand just where they are, my advice is to stay away from this field.

However, if you identify with kids and the way many of them think, then you're well aware that writing for kids is not writing down to them in any way. In an age when they are reading Jean Paul Sartre and Salinger—and at an age when, unfortunately, they are exposed to such things as *The Happy Hooker* and *Last Tango in Paris,* we have to understand that kids are aware of all sorts of material and are also reading in-depth material.

The most frequent mistake made in writing for Christian young people is that of underestimating them. Some years ago I was asked to help evaluate the books for young people of a Christian publishing house. We ended by taking the entire line of books and dropping them into three grades, because all the books had been projected for too old an audience. We ended having no books whatever for teenagers, having pushed those books to early junior high.

What is a book or article for a young person? Actually, it's in their interest range—yes—but it's simply good journalism applied to their interests. *Campus Life* recently selected books of particular interest to kids. Almost none of them were specifically aimed at kids. *The Hiding Place* took the top award, and yet it is a general book, not necessarily aimed at high schoolers.

At the same time, when you think of young people you have to realize that this is a large group broken into psychographic patterns. Kids range from those who want to do nothing all day but lie under the car and play with the grease, to the brainy type who is reading classical literature. In *Campus Life* we are trying to hit the broad cross section. We always aim to hit a minimum of 50 percent of these different types of readers with every article. At the same time we realize that adults are always reading over kids' shoulders, which further complicates things. As you write, think about these various types of people all reading the same article. The big job is to be able to hit all these people as thoroughly as possible.

How do you do that? Well, you pick one person whom you're speaking to—preferably a high school senior who is pretty aware of his world and is a Christian—and you speak directly to him. But it's as if you're talking in a coffee house to one person across the table, but a whole group of people are sitting around the table listening to your conversation. These are the people you don't want to alienate; these are the people you also want to communicate to.

You'll find tremendous blessings in writing for young people, because they are more malleable than the average adult. We get literally hundreds of letters from kids who have either accepted Christ through the magazine or find it their most important link in living a vibrant Christian life.

What specifics are we looking for? Well, we have a philosophy that the free-lancer must be the aggressive one to come up with the ideas. Often we're asked, "What do you want the articles written on?" We rely on the free-lancer to come up with ideas, with fresh subject matter and a unique approach. However, in broad terms we are always looking for articles which show how the Bible is changing the lives of kids in their everyday life, and also stories on activities kids are involved in. We suggest that instead of sending us a manuscript you send us a letter briefly outlining your idea. Then we can interact with you about whether or not it would work. This saves all of us a great deal of trouble.

We personally have no problem with multiple submissions: there are many good youth publications put out by denominations and publishing houses which use fiction and other stories similar to those in *Campus Life*. We don't feel there's much of an overlap. If you do sell something to another publishing house and want to send it to us with multiple submission written at the top, this is quite acceptable.

4
What Word Publishers Want

Floyd W. Thatcher
Vice-President and Executive Editor, Word Books

We are interested in manuscripts on virtually any subject area in the Christian arena with the exception of juvenile material—if it is carefully thought out and well-written. Specifically:

Biblical studies for the layman. These should not be larded with jargon. Assume your reader is intensely interested and excited by the Bible but is totally unfamiliar with "the language of Zion." The words of Jesus are excellent models for this type of writing. Books on biblical studies and topics engineered for both individual and small groups (house church) use are well received.

Personal stories. Experientially oriented books continue to evoke widespread interest. The author need not necessarily be well-known, but if he or she is not, the burden for innovation and craftsmanship in writing is extremely heavy.

Fiction. I would not have included this category until recently. But a survey we have taken does indicate an interest in good fiction; however, not the traditional and overtly "Christian" fiction that has appeared so often in the past. Probably what is wanted here was described pointedly in a conversation I had a year ago with Adela Rogers St. Johns on this very subject. She insisted that the writer's first obligation is to tell a good story—not set out to tell a good "Christian" story. Now, if the writer is a Christian, the story will naturally and effortlessly assume spiritual values. With this in mind, we can be interested in good fiction, but the story must speak for itself and not preach.

Biography. Good biography is a hot item on the so-called "secular" market. But most of what is selling is in the twentieth century setting. I'm convinced that good biography within the Christian orientation will be widely accepted. But, as with fiction, it must be a good story first—a story with integrity that is believable.

Marriage, family, and personal problems continue, I believe to be subjects of widespread interest and concern. To be both successful and helpful these must not be approached from a sweetness-and-light perspective. Rather I would urge that the earthiness of Jesus' approach in the Gospels be the model. People are hurting today, and plastic, superficial and pat answers not only fail to be of help but insult the intelligence of the reader who wants help.

New forms of the church and new dimensions of Christian expression. And I'm not talking here about something for pastors, but for the turned-on laymen or the one who desperately wants to be. We sense a somewhat astonishing aura of excitement about an authentic Christian faith and expression even among those organizationally disenchanted. To these, the cliches and "Protestant Latin" do not hack it and are totally meaningless. They want to know that somebody cares for and about them as persons. New and exciting ideas of how to witness and be God's people in the world always attract attention.

Finally, I think any Christian writer who is willing to pay the price for ideas and craftsmanship can sell—and we are certainly interested in him. This will require a turnaround from the mediocrity of most Christian writing of the past to an excellence which demands to be read. And in my mind, if we're deeply serious about the good news of Jesus Christ and the Christian gospel, we honestly can't do anything else.

5
Here's Union Gospel Press

T. T. Musselman, Jr.
Executive Vice-President, Union Gospel Press

Union Gospel Press is a nondenominational, fundamental, evangelical Christian publishing house. We have been publishing Bible-based literature for the Sunday school and the home for more than 70 years.

We are interested in free-lance material for all ages, particularly junior high through adult. All material *must* have an evangelical emphasis. We receive hundreds of submissions daily, but many are generally secular stories with a Scripture verse inserted in the conclusion. This is not acceptable. Our main purpose is to proclaim the gospel and to help born-again believers grow in their knowledge of Christ. Therefore, we are interested only in material that allows God's message to come through loud and clear. We want articles, stories, and poems that proclaim God's working in the lives of believers and that put forth the Lord's message of salvation.

Our material is departmentally graded; so writers should indicate the particular age group for which a manuscript is intended. A word count *must* be indicated on the first page of each manuscript. Depending on the type of selection being submitted, the word count may vary from 300 words to 2000 words. Queries as to our specific needs are welcome.

Writers should send only good, clean copy that has been double checked for spelling, punctuation and typing errors. We receive far too many stories, etc., that appear to have been rattled off in a matter of minutes. Often the basic themes are good, but the cohesion and development are poor, the typing sloppy and the factual data not referenced.

We would like to see more biographies of living people who are following God's Word, who have found comfort in the Lord during a crisis, or who are active in some Christian organization or group. We also welcome articles that discuss up-to-date topics such as abortion, women's lib, new trends in Christian education, youth movements, etc.

The most important point we can stress is that any submission must have a definite, clear-cut evangelical emphasis. We ask that writers not send us secular material that has been "doctored up" for religious publication. Instead, we would like those individuals who are interested in spreading God's Word to send us their best material to be used for His glory.

Part Two
You Work on Your Idea

6
Tips on Interviewing

James R. Adair
Power/Line Papers, Scripture Press

Interviewing is often the best part of the writing game apart from the sales and the checks that result. It can be tremendous fun. Interviews can bring you into personal contact with some of the most interesting people. Lifelong friendships can develop.

There is no need to dread interviews. Regardless of how great a person is, he's still human. And he's likely quite willing to share his views and accomplishments. Most people worth interviewing have little trouble talking, if you put them at ease. If you show genuine interest, your big problem might be to shut the interviewee off, or to keep him on track.

I must admit that, much like some speakers about to step to the podium, I have felt nervous about some interviews. But even as public speakers generally find that nervousness turns to satisfaction as they get going, my dreaded interviews have quickly developed into happy occasions.

The interviewer must enjoy people and be a good listener, much like a good conversationalist. Only recently I interviewed a charming woman who perhaps made a better interviewer than I. She had a way of talking to me about my experiences as if she really cared to hear what I had to tell her. She asked questions and maintained excellent eye contact. I knew she was thinking about what I was saying, for her expression showed it. I'm still not sure who got the best interview, though I'm sure I'll remember more of what she told me than what I told her—for I have a record of every single word she spoke.

You see, I depend on a tape recorder. I know there are experts who warn against poking a microphone in a person's face, for the person may freeze up and not be natural. But I've found that people I interview relax and forget the recorder when I explain that it's just for the sake of my poor memory. For years I've used reel-to-reel recorders, the latest one with automatic volume control, which helps to pick up softly-spoken words. More recently I've used cassette-type recorders. For transcribing, there are inexpensive foot-operated devices for stopping and starting the player.

For convenience, I hire a typist to transcribe the entire interview. But I have listened and typed out only what I really wanted. The former can get expensive, especially for a book, though the latter method takes a good chunk of the writer's own valuable time.

Many people successfully use shorthand or a form of it and take notes in a notebook. This is fine, especially if you can read your notes—and if you can do it and at the same time show interest in the person you are interviewing and not slow him down too much.

For some types of information, telephone interviewing is the answer. You can obtain a simple device to record a phone conversation—it costs about $3, plugs into a recorder, and suctions onto your phone.

Here are some tips for extensive interviews:

1. Phone or write for an appointment. Don't just barge in.

2. Plan your interview. Find out all you can about the person. This will help you plan pertinent questions. Write the questions down for easy referral.

3. Make sure that the person you are interviewing is planning adequate time. A rushed interview isn't worth a lot in most cases.

4. As you conduct the interview, show interest in your interviewee. Ask intelligent questions. Don't cut him off rudely when he wanders from the topic. Be courteous and respectful, for, after all, your interviewee is doing you a big favor.

7
Getting an Editor Interested

Let's suppose that while reading your newspaper the other morning you came across an interesting item on an inside page. The article told of the events leading up to the establishment of a Bible study group. Its uniqueness stemmed from the fact that it was led by a man well-known in the community as vice-president of the local bank. The article also appeared unusual from what he had to say about faith in Jesus Christ as being important to one's career and social life.

Smiting your brow with your hand, or whatever else you do when you get a great idea, you said, "This might make a good magazine article for *Christian Life, Campus Life* or *Faith at Work.*"

Easily you pictured how the article might look with your by-line. Equally simple it was to dream of the influence such a piece might be in opening doors of opportunity for people who might need advice or counsel on this subject.

Then you come down from cloud nine. "But how do I find out whether or not an editor would be interested in such an article?" you asked yourself.

If you are an experienced writer, you have discovered already that editors are eager to talk about article or book-length manuscript ideas. But only if you have researched the subject thoroughly enough to have become an expert on it and capable of convincing the editor that this would be a worthwhile piece for him to publish. After all, he is dependent upon writers for his livelihood, so he will encourage you whenever possible.

But you must do your homework before you visit or write an editor.

If you are conveniently enough located to visit the editor this simplifies the matter greatly. He is a busy man so you must make an appointment in advance. And if possible, have more than one idea to present. This way you give him the impression that his time with you was well spent—even if he does not accept all of your ideas.

Oftentimes, however, you will not be able to visit the editor personally. As a matter of fact, most magazine or book ideas are originally proposed by mail. What has become known as the "query letter" has become the standard procedure by which the writer feels out the editor's interest in the subject or subjects which he has in mind.

Here the procedures are rather standard. The purpose of a query letter is to sell your idea to the editor. He accepts such a letter for what it is—and actually, wants to be sold because he has editorial needs.

So your job is to present as many attractive aspects of your project as possible. Support these with evidence that you can come up with far more additional material equally as attractive and interesting. Obviously the best way to do this is to demonstrate in your letter that you have researched the subject thoroughly—not simply by saying so, but by the content of what you include in your letter.

You also will have studied the publication for which you are writing so that you can assure the editor that you will meet his needs: the proper length, adequate number of photographs, anecdotal material, etc., etc.

Finally, you should ask the editor for any suggestions that he may have which will make your piece more acceptable to him.

This may not sound necessary, but on the other hand editors would rather work with writers who are willing to take suggestions than with those who give the impression that their manuscript is the last word and that nothing can be done to improve it.

This kind of professional approach to an editor is bound to get you a sympathetic response. And remember, editors would far rather work with those who indicate a degree of professionalism than with the strict amateur.

In this connection, don't simply write a letter saying, "I would like to write an article on Mr. Dokes of the First National Bank. He is a friend of mine and I am sure he will give me a good interview." Such an approach smacks of the rankest kind of amateurism.

Similarly, a trip to Europe may be a great experience for you. But refrain from writing an editor saying that you are going to make such a trip and if he has any assignments you would be glad to handle them for him. Believe me, he won't. He expects you to make the suggestion which he can accept or reject.

Unlike manuscripts, it is not necessary to enclose an addressed stamped envelope with your query letter. This is a business transaction, and the editor does not expect you to pay the return freight.

The important thing to demonstrate in your approach to an editor—either personally or by mail—is that you are a reader of his books or publications. Therefore you understand what his needs are and are eager to help him meet them. He will respond to this kind of approach.

Part Three

You Put Your Idea into Its Best Form

8
How to Write Devotional Material

Wayne Christianson
Executive Editor, Moody Monthly

Many who submit manuscripts to Christian publications seem to be under the impression that devotional articles are the "Heavenly Hash" of religious journalism. They assume that the "devotional" is a catchall for lofty thoughts, sweet spiritual nothings and aimless flitting from cloud to cloud in a rosy haze of good intentions.

Most editors, I believe, would disagree. The devotional article is a firm—not flabby—piece of writing. It is solid, persuasive, well thought out. It is written to move the reader, not by exhorting or telling him what he should feel or do, but by *showing* him why and prompting him to do it.

Many types of articles—Bible studies, doctrinal articles, treatments on Christian living among others—have devotional qualities. But the devotional article per se is conceived and written purposefully to touch the heart for God and to help the reader in some very tangible way. Often it shares a personal discovery. Almost always it stresses spiritual priorities, deepens the reader's appreciation of the goodness and grace of God and strengthens his desire for all-out commitment to the Lord Jesus Christ.

Understandably the range of subject matter is virtually unlimited. You may write a devotional article on how God uses the irritations and frustrations of life to build character and faith; the therapy of thankfulness, even in the face of tragedy; the implications of being indwelled by the Holy Spirit. You may even find a theme which seems to invite a note of humor as did one writer who focused on the Christian's propensity to want to suffer in air-conditioned lions' dens.

With such a broad field before you, how do you choose a subject? Obviously you must find something worth saying. Your awareness of possible themes will depend on your Scripture intake, Christian experience, your awareness of what God is doing in the lives of others, your own desire for a closer walk with God. Obviously your prayer life and dependence on the Lord for a writing ministry will figure largely here.

When you have decided on a theme, think next about how you can best present it. Your approach must be fresh, appealing and convincing. At this point you will want to have your market well in mind. What publication is most likely to be interested in your basic theme? What types of development is the publisher using? What lengths? Unless you have the periodical's requirements clearly before you, refresh your memory before you decide on treatment.

In general there are several options. Suppose, for example, you want to show that the Christian faith leaves no room for fear (see Ps. 112:7; Rev. 21:8; etc.). You have considered the subject from every angle, gathered a file of anecdotes and related materials and now are ready to write.

One of the most simple and direct approaches is the anecdote-summary treatment often found in *Reader's Digest* articles on secular subjects. These introduce the theme by means of an effective anecdote, point up the principle involved and develop it by means of the anecdote-summary pattern. The reader is thus led toward a desired conclusion.

33

Or you may choose to develop your theme, at least in part, by sharing a personal experience—either yours or someone else's. (Be sure what you share will have interest and value to the reader.)

Don't ignore the possibility of an offbeat treatment—a letter format; a parable or fable; a short story, direct address approaching the point obliquely; creation of a mood as in some of the short features often found in *Campus Life*. Such offbeat slants take special skill, but often they are effective and appealing to an editor.

The important thing to keep in mind is that your reader is a person with a mind of his own: you can move him only when he is convinced that your way is the way to go. Don't preach; don't scold; don't tell him what he *ought* to do. Help him *want* to move your way by presenting facts, illustrations, relationships that will turn him in the right direction.

Often it helps to ask yourself, "What opened my eyes to this point I want to share?" The answer may help you decide how you can lead the reader through the same experience.

Should you use Scripture? Yes, of course, but seldom in terms of quoting lengthy portions. Point out and document principles. Avoid seeming to labor your points. Tell how you or others have been affected. In short, weave a tapestry of principle, experience, and the Scriptures.

You will find it helpful to watch for good devotional articles and read them carefully. Analyze them to learn what makes them good. Note what the writers have done and what they have avoided doing. Experiment in your own devotional writing. Practice.

Perhaps above all write with your reader in mind. You are ministering to him.

9
Poetry

Leslie Stobbe
Moody Press

Poetry provides the Christian with one of the most satisfying and exciting forms of self-expression. He can run the gamut of contemplative introspection, sharing of innermost thoughts, expressions of love, outrage, concern, awe and worship.

The rising tide of poetry flowing across the typical editor's desk confirms that Christians are utilizing such poetic expression as never before. God may have one of several purposes in mind for this expression.

Poetry may be a form of diary—a recording of life's experiences and the writer's reactions to them. Such poetic expression helps formalize our innermost feelings and provides an outlet for introspective reflection on the great purposes of life. We get to see who we really are.

On the other hand, poetry may be a commentary on life around us. This will reflect our sense of values and Christian convictions, while helping us to focus our response to life. Such commentary is a frequent feature of the Psalms.

Finally, poetry may be an expression of worship directed to our Creator and Redeemer. Instead of merely expressing our feelings and reactions, it expands on who God is—and His self-expression through Jesus Christ. The focus remains on the great God, rather than on ourselves. For the time being, heart and mind are filled with a paeon of praise that comes tumbling out in poetic form.

Unfortunately, too few poetic writers realize that God has given them this gift not necessarily for publication in book or magazine form. The poetry itself may be just as valuable to him under lock and key in his desk as a diary is to its owner. The writer has experienced life—and verbalized it in written form. In so doing he reaps genuine benefits even though they may appear intangible.

A select few will be chosen by God to communicate to a wider audience, just as not many preachers or teachers are called by the average congregation. These few may share their poetry at special occasions in the local church, the women's group of the club. Their contribution will be appreciated and it will touch lives. Others may be called to share their poetry with a denominational publication—and the only pay check will be a comment or two from friends or relatives.

Even less will be called to share their poetry with the broad mass of people represented by radio, books and magazines. The fact that friends or relatives encourage you does not necessarily mean you have been called by the Lord himself to have your poetry published. Nor is an inner compulsion to see your poetry in print necessarily evidence of God's call. Just as the Lord uses a church to call a preacher, so the Lord uses the public through an editor to "call" a poet into print.

The editor, for example, will be aware of changing tastes in poetic forms. Today the poet may write rhyming verse for his diary, but if he wants to be published he probably will express himself through free verse and focus on contemporary religious and social concerns. In fact, he may need to find an artist or photographer to illustrate his poetic expression before an editor will be willing to risk his publisher's capital.

Published collections of poetry may focus on a theme, respond to an event, or reflect a poet's experience of life. At all times he must reveal either deep sensitivity to beauty, inner conflict and victory, concern or judgment of contemporary expressions of life. The poet must experience more deeply, respond with greater concern, or react more vividly to rise above the everyday reactions of his peers. He must represent the ultimate in human awareness, concern and sharing to be read today and he must be filled with the Holy Spirit to communicate God's grace and mercy revealed through Jesus Christ.

10
How to Write How-To-Do-It Articles

Eleanor Doan
Special Projects and Information,
Gospel Light Publications

The purpose of the how-to-do-it article is instructional. When properly written it can be said, "If you can read it you can do what it says."

This is evident in how-to-do-it articles found in Scripture: "How to Build the Tabernacle in the Wilderness" (Ex. 25:1-27:21), "How to Build the Temple" (II Chron. 3:3-4:22), "How to Become a Christian" (Romans 10:9,10). These "articles" also exemplify application of the basic principles for good how-to article writing, which merit careful observation.

Today's "instant living" lifestyle is dependent upon "how-to" articles—travel tips, recipes, investments, tax savings, decorating, camping tips, handcrafts, sewing, job procurement, hobbies, lesson preparation, teaching tips, use of teaching aids, witnessing, etc.—and a standard of excellence is necessary if the reading enables the doing. In striving for excellence, the following guidelines are basic.

BEFORE WRITING

1. *Determine the purpose* of the article—in writing. Keep in mind that the purpose should be made obvious by the title and the lead statement. Create a positive impression of benefits and confidence of achieving success.

2. *Outline the article,* giving careful attention to logical sequence. Develop each step on a 4x6" card. Make revisions required after observing the following point.

3. *Experience the "doing"* before writing the "how-to-ing," making notes on the cards. Test each step for clarity, practicality, results.

4. *Determine if illustrations* (drawings, diagrams, charts, photos, etc.) are necessary for clarity. Indicate at which point(s) reference should be made to them.

5. *Keep the reader in mind* at every point of planning. Do not take for granted he can learn from generalities. Be specific. Leave nothing to his imagination. Do not overestimate his knowledge; do not underestimate his intelligence.

WRITING THE ARTICLE

1. *Think through the entire article* and write clearly, in logical order.

2. *Write concisely,* making every word count. Be specific so as to lead the reader-doer to achievement.

3. *Strive for unity* in the article development with an interest-inviting style and sequential development.

4. *In a concluding summary* lead the reader-doer to realize that he has experienced satisfaction in achievement and the resulting usefulness of the article as set forth in the lead statement of purpose.

5. *Revise the article* to your satisfaction. Then have someone objectively test it. If he can read it and do what it says, then you will know it is right!

11
Writing for the Charismatic Market

Viola Malachuk
Logos International

Every week at *Logos* I face a formidable pile of unsolicited manuscripts. Most are accompanied by a letter urging us to publish the piece with the fewest possible alterations. Many claim some kind of divine inspiration and virtually demand that we acknowledge an infallability in what has been written. How is one to judge such things?

As I read the covering letter there is one thing I am looking for: does it reflect a broken spirit in the author, or is it an ultimatum? The chronic problem of Pentecost is the assumption that revelation and spiritual gifts indicate personal merit in the receiver. The primary qualification for good writing aimed at the charismatic market is a contrite heart—emerging from a realization of one's own wickedness and uncleanness before God. In short, the message is not, " I speak in tongues," but "Jesus is Lord."

I'm also looking for freshness and readability. If you are going to explain the meaning of some passage of Scripture to me, it would help to have a story from your own life or another's that will clearly illustrate your point. And if you do have such a story, is it original or am I likely to have already heard it? Is your writing clear, direct and simple? The ability to write well usually does not come automatically with the Baptism of the Holy Spirit; it must be learned.

The majority of our bestsellers are autobiographical testimonies that, although they report miracles of healing, financial supply and the like, basically tell how the author came to experience brokenness before God. Their own stories contain fresh data that dramatically illustrate and, at the same time, revive a specific truth of Scripture that the Holy Spirit wants to bring to the attention of the Church.

What every charismatic writer needs is a friend who will be friend enough to give serious critical appraisal of his or her work. Nothing is so valuable in producing good writing or, for that matter, good Christian character. Pray for such a friend—and don't overlook the obvious answer to that prayer—it could be the one from whom you least want to hear the truth, like your husband or wife.

Here are some questions that your friend will help you answer:

1. Why are you writing this?

2. Have you done your research so that you are thoroughly acquainted with your subject?

3. Does what you have written meet specific current needs in the body of Christ and the world?

4. Has someone already covered the subject better than you can?

5. Will what you have written create understanding or cause confusion?

6. What purpose do the sensational aspects of your story serve?

7. Finally, and most importantly, who will be exalted by your writing? (There is a thin line, as Charles Simpson puts it, between bragging and testifying.)

It is easy to see that writing for the charismatic market is not a task that one lightly undertakes. To be a charismatic writer, one must combine technical and professional competence with a willingness to write what the Lord wants written. This can be costly. True, there will be miracles to report, and heart-lifting stories of the Lord's mighty works among His people. But there will also be the story of God's chastisement in one's own life—and it is never pleasant to tell of *that.* In short, if one is called to be a charismatic writer, there can be no room for pride or self-seeking. But that means that there will be plenty of room for the joy that always follows when one is doing the perfect will of the Lord.

12
Juveniles Have Problems, Too

Mary Powell
Acting Director, Christian Writers Institute

You've decided you'd like to write fiction for children. You feel that winning a child to the Lord or helping one grow into a strong Christian has more lasting worth than the same done for an adult because you don't know what a blessing to the world the child may become.

Only the best is good enough; a child, like an adult, will not read a story that doesn't hold his interest.

Years ago some writers felt that anyone could "write a sweet little story for children." But children have changed—or maybe they haven't!—and they don't like "sweet little stories—yeech."

Preschoolers learn math and reading; third graders learn about the planets and can discuss the problems of space travel; sixth graders are starting on algebra. So it's easy to understand why they don't like a story that talks down to them.

Probably the most important thing to remember in writing for children is that there should be a problem in every story—and it should be a real one.

Even young children have problems. What do they do when older kids gang up on them? How do they know the Bible is true? That God really can help?

A youngster, under two years of age, overheard his mother discussing Christ's crucifixion with an older child. A couple of days later she said something about Jesus helping people. This "baby" said, "How can He help anybody? He's just a dead man." Of course, it was explained to him that Jesus rose from the dead but this same youngster, several years older now, said recently, "I know the Bible says it's true and you say that God can do anything, but it's still hard to believe." And in how many other children's hearts is this same doubt?

What about such a simple thing as accepting Christ? A child knows a person can't actually get inside his beating heart even though people tell him to let Jesus come into his heart. What do these grownups really mean? And kids learn in school that their heart stays the same color so how can it turn from black to white? Even though they may want to love God will they grow spiritually if they don't quite understand or believe what they've been told?

What about the older child? The 11 or 12-year-old. The one in Junior Hi. He may be a Christian but He probably has times of wondering if God really knows he's around—does God really order his life? Or what about witnessing? How can he be a witness? The results usually are discouraging. One eighth grader said, "Mom, all the articles and stories in the Sunday school papers make it sound like kids are hungry for the Gospel. But in real life it doesn't work out that way. You talk about God and they either shrug or change the subject. It's rough."

Of course, every problem doesn't have to be *big*. Making friends in a new school or even getting money for something special can be a problem. After you have a real problem, *be sure the solution is believable.* Very seldom, in real life, does the memory of a Scripture verse solve a problem for a youngster. So think hard before you have it work that way for a story youngster. The work in writing for children is to come up with a fresh, believable, helpful solution.

Sometimes your climax won't be happy. Maybe nobody, no way, is interested in the Lord from the witness of the young person. But he might somehow realize that he's grown spiritually from trying to put into words what he believes. Just because a witness doesn't see results doesn't mean that he hasn't accomplished anything.

This kind of writing takes time—and thought. Every part must dovetail into every other part. It's rewarding though—if a youngster likes your work, he'll notice who wrote it. He'll read everything you write and he'll believe the things you say.

Adults may read your writing because of the intriguing way you express yourself without thinking much about your message. Kids are most interested in what you say.

13
Vacation Bible School Material

Milford S. Sholund
Vice-President for Publications,
Gospel Light Publications

Writing Vaction Bible School materials is challenging and rewarding. Challenging because these materials must be attractive, biblical, simple, concise and practical. Rewarding because the spectrum of ages goes all the way from two years to old age with a potential audience of more than 9,000,000 students and workers participating every year. If you are thinking of writing Vacation Bible School material, you have an unlimited opportunity.

The first requirement in writing for this audience is to understand what Vacation Bible Schools are all about. The typical VBS is a short-term program of evangelism and Christian education. Usually there are about 30 hours of activities spread over a period of two weeks. There are many schools that are limited to 15 hours in one week and a few that go for more than 30 hours over a period of three or four weeks. The important thing to remember is that it is a highly-concentrated effort involving volunteer teachers and workers heavily dependent on the written material for their instruction and guidance in the programming.

The thrust of a typical VBS is two-fold: evangelism and education. Many churches find VBS to be one of the greatest means of reaching people in the community. Churches often report as much as 50% of the VBS enrollment coming from families whose members have not confessed Christ as Savior and Lord. The educational thrust is usually concentrated on biblical themes and characters in the framework of two to three hours of teaching/learning activities. A VBS with 10 days of three hours per day can often concentrate on a total educational impact that rivals the influence of the Sunday school.

The teaching/learning activities of the VBS are usually diversified to involve student participation in activities for the whole student. There is something to hear in the stories and instruction; there is something to see in banners, posters, pictures, movies; there is something to feel in the use of scissors, tools, handwork, craft materials and various objects; there is something to taste in refreshments and goodies and there is something to do in combining all of these sensory activities. A well-directed VBS can have a very satisfying, wholesome, impact on students of all ages.

If you want to write for VBS, you will keep in mind then the totality of all these experiences and how the various materials dovetail to help the students, the teachers and the leaders as they all work together. The written materials for the typical VBS include: teacher's manuals, student's books, teaching resources, craft activities and promotional materials.

The heart of the teacher's manual is the biblical message usually in story form. The selection of Bible stories should be geared to the interest and understanding of the typical age group for whom it is intended. Vacation Bible Schools are often developed for pre-kindergarten, ages 2 and 3; kindergarten, ages 4 and 5; primary, grades 1 and 2; middler, grades 3 and 4; junior, grades 5 and 6; junior high, grades 7 and 8; youth, high school grades; and adults. It is obvious that if one is to write Bible stories for VBS one must choose the area in which he has ability to develop the story in a way that is useful and worthwhile for the typical age group. The story should be true to the Bible but it can be embellished with description, narration, dialogue, and drama. Since the typical VBS teacher is a volunteer, the development of a Bible story by a writer can make the difference between success and mediocrity in helping the teacher convey what the Bible teaches. The typical story should not be more than 2,000 words since the teacher would usually only be involved in the storytelling for 10 to 15 minutes.

The student's books should be designed to involve the student in meaningful, relevant ideas and activities which help him develop the thrust of the Bible story. This takes some imagination and very often the publisher will have the student's material developed by the staff. However, publishers often want ideas on layout and format and art and interesting suggestions on developing a student's book. In addition to the booklet the student develops for himself, there is a need for Bible games, supplementary reading materials, pamphlets, books and flat pictures. Publishers are often looking for new ideas that make the Bible live for students who are seldom stimulated by exciting presentations of the Bible. In view of the impact of TV, radio, sports, travel and colorful literature, the writer is really challenged to come up with something that is exciting and meaningful for the student. However, the privilege of making Christ known in this generation is worth every ounce of effort.

Teaching resources are supplementary materials that teachers and students use to reinforce the Bible truth. Resources may include: charts, posters, flannelboard stories, chalkboard drawings, filmstrips, slides, movies, skits, and other materials that will assist the teacher in guiding the student in a better understanding of the message from the Lord. The writer who wants to get involved in this assortment of opportunities should confer with the publisher about his needs. Obviously, there is almost an unlimited possibility of participating in the development of VBS materials if one has imagination and artistic capabilities.

Craft activities are often incorporated into the VBS program. Some crafts are complete in a box and only need to be put together by the students. Some crafts are developed from the creative abilities of the students stimulated by ideas that are given in written form. There is always the question of whether or not crafts should necessarily be coordinated with the Biblical and religious significance or if it can be more practical. The answer is that the typical craft involvement probably should have some of both features. Students generally enjoy the craft involvement because it allows them to make something which they can enjoy and in many instances they can take home and have as a useful reminder of happy days of VBS. Publishers welcome ideas on craft activities. They will pay for these ideas when they are developed in written form with precise instructions on how to create the crafts. One of the most demanding requirements in writing for craft ideas is the need for clarity and specific instructions on how to prepare and make the crafts. It is amazing how difficult it is to write instructions for someone else to understand. Again, the writer must always bear in mind that when he does a good job some child, youth or adult will be grateful he had a chance to do something which was successful and satisfying.

Writing promotional materials involves many areas including newspaper articles, photographs of personnel and students, posters for advertising, mimeographed instructions for various events and closing programs. Many schools lose the maximum opportunities for making Christ known to the community by failure to develop promotional materials that are different, exciting, complete and specific in their messages to the public. There is also the opportunity of developing announcements and scripts to be used on local radio stations and TV interviews. Many churches have aroused curiosity by developing parades involving children and young people riding tricycles, bicycles, wagons, walking with pets, festooned with balloons, banners and other gear. Promotional materials are important for use in many Vacation Bible Schools since there seems too often to be a lack of appreciation and imagination in developing awareness of the significance of the VBS in a community.

An inevitable question comes to a person who wants to write for VBS. For whom do I write and where do I send my materials? There are three options: (1) Write for your own church. (2) Write for your denomination. Inquire from the Christian Education office of your denomination about their plans for the next two to five years. (3) Write to trans-denominational publishers including: Gospel Light Publications, 110 W. Broadway, Glendale, CA 91209; Scripture Press, 1825 College Ave., Wheaton, IL 60187; Concordia Publishing House, 3558 S. Jefferson Ave., St. Louis, MO 63118; and Standard Publishing, 8121 Hamilton Ave., Cincinnati, OH 45231.

Writing VBS materials can be challenging as one tries to make the Bible live today. It can be rewarding, by faith, as one realizes that Christ is using these materials in the hands of students and teachers and it can be worthwhile financially when the written material is accepted for publication.

Write on for VBS!

Part Four
An Editor Sees
Your Manuscript

14
The Necessity of Editorial Changes

Kenneth L. Wilson
Editor, Christian Herald

Some of my best friends are writers. And I think—or hope—all of my best writers are friends. I find that the less professional the writer, the more sensitive he or she is likely to be about necessary copy changes. The more professional the editor, the more he strives to preserve the style of the writer and to keep himself and his own style out of the picture. The best editing is the least. The best editing is that which allows the writer to be at his best, that helps him to say intelligibly what he intended to say. The editor is the one on whom an author tries an idea for size. What may seem perfectly clear to the writer may not be clear to the reader. The editor is the prototype reader, not the omniscient judge.

I think the most satisfying comment I received after publication of an article was the writer's note: "Thank you for letting me appear in public with a clean face."

Writing is not only using the right words. It is style, rhythm, emotion, movement—any of which may be as important or even more important than the meaning of the assemblage of words. The editor tries to keep this in mind. He tries to put himself into the mind of the writer, not to strain the writer through his own mind.

The editor is a privileged person. He becomes privy to the most sacred and personal thought of many people—for often it takes courage to commit ideas to paper. He must respect and treat gently what is entrusted to him. Writing and editing are holy offices.

15
What Creation House Looks For

Dr. Robert Webber
Editor-in-Chief, Creation House

What does a book editor look for in a manuscript? Perhaps you have asked yourself this question over and over again as you have tried to second-guess people like me. Let me share some insights which might be helpful.

The first thing I do is look at *the idea*. What is this manuscript all about? What is its central thrust—or does it even have one? Does it zero in on a matter of specific interest? Is it a current subject? Have a number of books on this subject appeared in the past year? Have we already published a book on this subject?

These are crucial questions. A manuscript containing a good idea may be rejected because the market is saturated with books on the same subject. Or, your idea may be new and you may need to sell an editor on it. In this case, I suggest you include a prospectus answering the above questions. This would show an editor that you had done your homework, that you knew the audience and potential contribution of your book. Editors are not infallible. They need to know the market for an idea. Any help you can provide is appreciated.

My second move is to examine *the development of the idea.* I'm a reader like everyone else. Does the author get me into his work? Does the idea flow naturally? Does the writer gather up the loose ends? Have all my questions been answered?

Also, I am interested in knowing how the idea affects me as I encounter it. I don't want to be held at arm's length from the subject; I want to be drawn in a personal and attached way. In a detached piece of writing, the reader always stays outside looking at the subject. It doesn't affect him personally. In a personal piece of writing the reader is drawn into the work in such a way that the material examines him.

Finally I'm concerned about *the clarity of the idea.* Does the writer have a clear notion of what he's trying to say? Does he say it simply and directly? I remember some homiletical advice I was given by a seasoned preacher. He said, "Have something to say; stand up and say it; sit down." I think the same advice is good for writers. When you have something to say, say it! Don't air your ideas in a jumble of words. Words are only vehicles for ideas. When words become more important than an idea, the idea gets lost.

These are a few of the major items I look for in an incoming manuscript. Naturally, every editor is slightly different from the next. I can't speak for other editors, but I think most would agree on the things I have suggested.

16
Your Mss. Will Look Like This

After your manuscript has been accepted by an editor your work is finished, but the editor's has begun. It's his job to make your article or story better but let it remain *your* work.

Here are four pages of an edited manuscript. The article appeared in *Christian Life* magazine.

On page 1, the author should have begun the article half way down the page with the title and her by-line under it. Although it isn't shown on these reproduced sheets, the author used real names; these were changed by the editor. In this type of article fictitious names should be used.

In the third paragraph, it wasn't clear where she was teaching—it might have been a private Christian school or even a Sunday school. The reader has no way of knowing.

On page 2 the editor has made the article more concise and lively by careful editing.

On page 3, about half way down the page, the author slips from past tense to present tense. The editor has changed these places. Usually past tense is best but whatever style you use should be consistent throughout the manuscript.

On page 4 notice how the editing improves the article. Also try to follow the style of the target publication—notice how *Christian Life* prefers the title of books.

When an editor works on your manuscript he's not doing it because he feels it isn't good (if he hadn't liked it he wouldn't have bought it) but because an author and an editor together make an unbeatable team.

Betty Reid
Hillcrest Apts. 4
Dowagiac, MI 49047

About 2000 words

THE EXCITEMENT OF TEACHING

The handwriting ~~THE DOOR IS STILL OPEN~~ *was awkward, the query sincere:*

"Miss Reid, I've never been able to ask a teacher before, but ↓ you tell me what you think of pre-marital sex."

I stared down at Susie's carelessly-written journal with surprise. *This* ↓sterous eighth-grade ~~Susie~~ seldom ~~showed she could have such~~ *revealed a* ↓ous thought~~s~~.

Yet I was ~~very~~ glad to ~~see Susie's~~ *read her* honest ~~query for~~ *request.* It meant ↓t after a semester of journal writing the one-to-one relation- ↓p between teacher and student ~~us as public school)~~ was beginning to pay off. ~~This~~ ~~stion of~~ Susie's *question* showed her ability to trust me with the most sonal *part of* in her life. *to write*

With a little prayer I began my answer. "I could give you many ↓sons against pre-marital sex: emotional hangups, veneral disease, unwanted pregnancy. However, to make it personal, I must make ↓ religious. I am a Christian. The Bible says that Christians ↓uld not engage in pre-marital sex, therefore, I do not.

"You, of course, must make your own decision. Take your time, ↓ie. ~~and~~ Make it wisely."

↓ I often find myself amazed as I hear people speak of the lack ↓ ability to witness in the public schools. ~~It seemed that~~ When ↓ Supreme Court decision on prayer was made, *many* people thought that ↓ hope was lost. Yet this verdict ~~may have~~ *has* opened the way for ↓h more meaningful witness~~ing~~ by Christians teachers.

2

After this ruling, the Bible was brought into schools as part
of literature courses. When I taught Fantasy Literature last
semester, I was able to spend a week teaching the Bible. After we
had finished studying Greek mythology, I pointed out to
my students that they would meet Bible characters as often as Greek
heroes in literature and that they needed to be aware of them.

We did not have a textbook for this part of the course so I told
the Bible stories and used supplimental material the book GOD IS FOR REAL,
MAN, by Carl Burke. In this setting, I got my
witness across by my choice of words, emphasis on certain
stories and my implicit belief.

We discussed the Bible freely and I soon discovered that
one needed to be prepared for more unexpected
opportunities.

One day I assigned a story called "Satan and Sam Shay" In it, a
clever Irishman outwits the devil. I expected limited
discussion because this particular class was slow to participate. However
as the period began I found myself bonbarded by questions.

"Miss Reid, is there really a devil?"

"How do we know that heaven is good and hell is bad? That's just
what we've been told."

"There's nothing wrong with a ouija board, is there?"

"Wait a minute," I broke into the babble of voices. "If you
raise your hands and ask your questions one at a time we can all
hear them." My mind was a whirling. Shades of Christian apologetics!
Where were all those answers I'd sought for myself so many years
ago?

"Okay, Donna, what's your question?"

"My family is Catholic but my brother has turned Buddhist and
the leader of his group. He taught me a Buddhist chant to say
I was in trouble. I believe in God but it's all right to be-
ve in Buddha too, isn't it?"

"Donna, I have to go back to the Bible," I said slowly. "One of the
Commandments say, Thou shalt have no other god's before me. ~~If~~
you worship someone other than God, it's called idoltry."

"But I don't believe in Buddha in that way."

"Then why do you chant?"

Another hand was raised and Pam spoke, "I believe in rein-
nation. Each time I'm reborn, I get better."

"Many people believe in reincarnation, "I responded, "But as you
ok around at people today, do they seem to be getting ~~better and~~
ter? They should after so many rebirths, shouldn't they?"

"Yes but..." Her voice faded.

"Again Pam, I have to go back to the Bible for an answer. It says in the book of Hebrews, verse 27, 'It is
pointed unto men once to die, but after this the judgment was.'"

"Miss Reid, can you really prove there's a God?" Jon is quick
fill in the short silence.

"No, Jon, we can point to evidences of God but we can't prove
s existence. We must accept Him, by faith."

"Miss Reid," petite Mary began very deliberately. "How do we
ow that Christianity is the best religion? We always look down
Hinduism and Buddhism and I don't think we should. How do we
ow which religion is best?"

As I paused before answering, ~~in trying to answer this question~~ my thoughts seemed to travel in many directions. "Mary," ~~I wondered,~~ "is it really you ~~who is~~ asking this question? I thought ~~that~~ you were on pretty firm footing. You shared with me in your journal that you'd had a real experience with God at a Catholic retreat, and I'd rejoiced with you. Then ~~You asked if I'd laugh at the thought of your becoming a nun. I assured you that i wouldn't and~~ shared with you the book MARIA ~~to show you that~~ in which if vivacious, ~~slightly undisciplined~~ Maria von Trapp ~~could become a nun so could you~~ came to know God personally.

"Lord, help me to reassure her faith," I prayed silently.

"One big difference, Mary, is that in Christianity, God reached down to man and offered him salvation and eternal life. In other religions a man has to struggle to find God. ~~and~~ He can never be sure that he has found Him as he can in Christianity."

"But what about Satan and witchcraft?" Joe interjected before I could go on. "Do you believe in them?"

"Yes," I stated, "Western society once thought Satan was a myth, but now there are churches ~~who~~ which worship him. Witchcraft goes right along with this. It's dangerous and should be left alone." The look of disbelief enter~~ed~~ the eyes of several students so I ~~make the plea,~~ said, "At least look at both sides before you get involved in it."

The bell prevent~~ed~~ further questions. However, ~~tomorrow is another day and~~ I ~~will bring in reading material,~~ made a mental note to bring material to class articles by former Satan worshiper Michael Warnke; Paul Little's book, KNOW WHY YOU BELIEVE; and SCREWTAPE LETTERS, by C.S. Lewis. Because I am in ~~the~~ a public school, I ~~will~~ would merely make these materials available to my students and let them decide whether or not to read them.

Such class sessions are highlights. They ~~come only occasionally. and~~ It is my students'

Part Five
It Comes Back

17
What to Do With a Rejection Slip

Robert Walker
Editor, Christian Life

Every writer receives rejection slips. But not every writer knows what to do with them.

Some writers cry over them. Others become angry. Many simply throw them into the wastebasket and try to forget them. One writer once led me into his study to show me what he did with them. All four walls and the ceiling were papered with them.

Whatever your reaction may be to a rejection slip, the important thing is to learn from it.

If you have received a rejection letter instead of a rejection slip then you should read carefully what the editor has to say. He has taken the time to write you and probably because he would like to use the manuscript if you could make the necessary changes in it. So instead of resenting the fact that the manuscript has been returned, consider carefully how you may make the additions he has asked for, cut or rewrite in order that the manuscript may have a better chance of being accepted when you return it.

But suppose you have received no letter—only a cold, impersonal rejection slip. What then?

Probably the best thing to do is to reconsider the subject on which you have written: is it timely, is it significant enough, have you included adequate anecdotal material and does it conform to the general style of the publications to which you have sent it? Reviewing a check list like this may give you some important insights as to how the manuscript might be rewritten before it is sent out again.

And even before you do that, consider again the possibility of querying several editors on the subject before you submit the manuscript. This way you may get help in advance from the editor as to how he would like to have the manuscript slanted to reach his market. Also, he will be alerted that a manuscript from you is on the way. Even a little preparation like this can pave the way for a more friendly reception.

Finally, always remember that as a writer one of the occupational diseases that you will suffer from is discouragement. This means that you should take every precaution to try to avoid dry spells. That is, times when you become discouraged and give up on your writing. This not only results in frustration, but lack of productivity.

A secret which I discovered in my free-lancing days to avoid periods of discouragement was to keep three or four manuscripts in process at all times. Some ideas would be in the research stage. Others would be out on the query basis. Some would be in the writing process. And others, actually in the marketing stage and in the hands of editors.

But here is a caution. There is no reason why you cannot query three or four editors at the same time. Then when their replies come in you select the market which you think you have the best chance at making or where you would like to see your manuscript published. If it is accepted, then simply write those who indicated their willingness to consider the manuscript and explain that the manuscript has been marketed but that you will query them about other subjects in the future.

On the other hand, if you get a rejection from the first publication, then without waiting for a response to another query, you can send it out to the second market. This way you keep the manuscript moving and avoid the periods when you might become discouraged because of a rejection slip or because of a long wait for a response from an editor.

But never. And I repeat, *never* send the same manuscript to two different publishers simultaneously. This is the mark either of an ignorant writer or of an unethical one. And since neither label is complimentary, you will want to avoid both.

Sure, you are going to get rejection slips or rejection letters. But let them become stepping stones to success and you will regard them in another light. This is what to do with them.

Part Six

Remember
the Nitty-Gritty

18
That Magic Ingredient: Dialogue

Jan Franzen
Executive Editor, Christian Life

Dialogue in a story or article comes close to being a magic ingredient. It forwards the action, shows conflict, delineates a person's temperament and character, conveys emotion, builds suspense, foreshadows the future (trouble, etc.), gives information. And it does all this in such a way that the reader is involved in the situation and caught up in the story.

Yet, as an editor, I've discovered that most authors neglect, or overlook, the importance of dialogue. Instead of showing characters talking, they prefer to describe what was said.

This is deadly.

But there is a way to *think* dialogue when writing either fiction or nonfiction. The secret: plan your manuscript in scenes, preferably in scenes of conflict. *Show* the problem. You'll soon discover that you cannot do this without the use of dialogue. *Show* the character in significant action. Again you'll discover that you cannot do this without including conversation between persons.

Here are some additional tips:

* Learn to listen. Notice that doctors, teachers, lawyers, bricklayers and truck drivers speak differently. Each has his own vocabulary; his own speech pattern.

* Learn to be selective. As a writer, you should rarely, if ever, give dialogue just as you heard it. You must interpret; must notice not only what was said, but how it was said. You must give the swing, the pacing of each person's speech.

* Learn to handle dialect. Don't go overboard on dropping "g's" for example. Usually the inclusion of an occasional speech oddity will be enough.

* Learn to handle speech keys (he said, he demanded, etc.). Remember that you cannot "laugh" a sentence.

* Learn to intersperse conversation with action, reaction, interaction.

* Learn to be consistent. Although a person changes his speech somewhat, depending upon to whom he is speaking, or where he is speaking, the reader should be able to see that changes are not too abrupt. Sentence length usually follows a pattern.

The Bible says (Matthew 12:34) that "out of the abundance of the heart, a man speaketh." So dialogue is truly an indication of what a man is "inside." You can, therefore, individualize your characters by what they say.

Dialogue also should make the reader feel strongly about a character. If you're using dialogue in an anecdote, to show the reader the significance of the subject of your article, be sure that he says something that will highlight the characteristic you want to use as the "thread" of your article: perseverance, compassion, generosity, etc. If you're using dialogue in an opening scene in a true adventure, make it show conflict, suspense, and/or foreshadow the future. And if you're using dialogue in a short story, make sure it accomplishes *at least* one of the seven purposes mentioned in the first paragraph of this article.

Remember—the more of these purposes your dialogue performs, the better, for it will make your manuscript more interesting, more significant, and more artistic.

19
How to Use This Book

This book can help you to become a better writer.

Most of the editorial material is written by editors to give you the editor's slant on various types of writing. Read it carefully.

There are about 250 markets listed. Roman Catholic magazines and book publishers are listed separately because there are different slants and taboos for them then for Protestant publications.

Read the listings of those publications for which you'd like to write. Then send for market guides and sample copies. Enclose 25¢, or stamps, unless the listing says their material for writers is free. When the samples arrive, study them carefully. Each publication has a different slant; find out what it is and write for it when you send a manuscript to your target publication.

Be sure your manuscript is typed on one side of a sheet, double-spaced. Your name and address should be in the upper left-hand corner of the first page, the approximate number of words in the upper right. The title comes about a third of the way down that first page with your by-line under it. It's best to use your own name. The top of each of the other pages of the manuscript should have the page number plus your name *or* the name of the story or article. You can paper clip the pages together; don't staple.

And send a self-addressed, stamped envelope for the return of the manuscript in case it's rejected.

If you have an idea for a full-length article (or a book) do query the editor to see if he's interested in seeing the completed article. A go-ahead letter from the editor doesn't mean the manuscript will be accepted, however. Don't query about articles under 1200 words unless the publication specifically says to. Never query about fiction.

And never, never send the same manuscript to more than one editor at a time.

Happy writing.

Part Seven

To Help You
Be a Better Writer

20
Writers' Conferences

Ruth McKinney
Decision

"Seek great teachers and sit under their tutelage, not to admire but to study." I'm not sure who first wrote that, but it is good advice for beginning writers.

"Great teachers" have been coming to Minneapolis for three days each summer since 1963 to participate in *Decision* magazine's annual School of Christian Writing. Editor Sherwood E. Wirt first conceived the idea of such a school after attending Robert Walker's Christian Writers Institute conference at Wheaton, Illinois, in 1961.

I have been on the staff of *Decision's* school since its inception. I have seen that the basis for our school has been the authority of the Scriptures. As one of the speakers said, "If the Bible is not the source for your writing, you are not doing Christian writing." The goal in Minneapolis—and at other Christian writers conferences—has been not only better writing, but better writing that will change lives.

72

Dr. Wirt set the tone for our goals in one of his early lectures. "We are not here to entertain you," he said, "we are here to get you into print. That's our business and we're not fooling around. We expect you to get yourself under the discipline of the writer which means writing something every day. And we expect you to produce—not for us, but for Jesus Christ."

My own claim to writing, before the first *Decision* school, was letters beginning "thanks for yours of May 25th . . . ." Letters are still my main job, but even *I* have been motivated to experiment with the creative written word. I want to go beyond the biographical and news articles published in our little interoffice paper *Our Decision* and to do more than update the missionary brochures of our church.

The best results of any writing conference show up in the accomplishments of its alumni. Since I serve as editorial secretary of *Decision,* many of the results of our schools have passed across my desk. Clippings describing the writing conferences, complete with pictures, are sent in by students whose reports are published by their local papers. Many of their articles appear in our magazine. Books authored by our students are increasing in numbers.

Rosanne E. Nelson, an alumna of our 1972 school, sums up the value of a Christian Writing School in her "thank you" letter dated November 28, 1972:

> Your school offered much encouragement, and I left there with a more realistic approach to the whole idea of writing. I realized it took work, discipline and setting priorities. Your school also offered something else—an opportunity to meet editors. And I did meet an editor—Mr. Alex Liepa of Doubleday.
>
> For about a year I had been working on a book. I shared my idea with Mr. Liepa while there—and he liked it. When I completed my manuscript—about two months ago—I sent it to him. And lo and behold—Doubleday is going to publish my book!
>
> In three days you can't teach a person to write. But it was the experience of just being there—around other writers, editors, and gathering information, that to me was a God-send. Thank you. (Rosanne's book, *Dear Jesus . . . I'm So Human,* published by Doubleday, September 1973.)

Mrs. Nelson is correct when she says that a writing conference of three days cannot teach us how to write. But it can teach us what to do with our writing. It can help us get ideas for writing. We can learn how to tighten and edit manuscripts and how to present them to the editors. We can learn where the markets are and how to fit our writings to their needs. A writing conference can also teach unselfishness in writing. We learn to stop writing for ourselves and to write for others.

Above all, we obtain the necessary knowledge to see ourselves in print—as writers!

21
Combining the Visual Arts with the Written Word

Marie Chapian
Author of City Psalms *and* Mind Things

Have you ever thought of coupling your writing talents with artistic expression?

We are in an age now of visiual communication, and we are accustomed to receiving visual artistic impressions every day. Advertising art in its myriad forms confronts us from all directions, and the major visual influence on our lives is the television screen. This has a serious effect on the writer and his work, unless he is an advertising copy writer or a television script writer.

A visually-oriented culture such as ours can be of great benefit to the Christian author in his ministry of reaching souls for the Lord. It is this idea I want to explore with you.

Your writing might adapt perfectly with visual expression, and if it does, you will want to examine the many possibilities there are available for you to choose from.

75

Let's narrow these artistic possibilities down to two forms: *photography* and *art.*

For the most part, the writer does not do the job of an art director, but he must understand certain principles necessary for producing a literary product utilizing both visual art and the written word.

How do you begin? First, look over the manuscript and discover where there is pictorial emphasis in the writing. Look for visual identification. Writing has a point of view, and so must the art which accompanies it. If you're beginning the work, use the same tactic. Scrutinize.

Does the written message need to have visual expression? How can you decide whether or not a work stands well enough alone, or whether it might meet with deeper response if visuals are added? In discovering the answers to these questions, it is necessary to investigate the following principles of communication: *the technique, the aesthetics* and *the message.*

Let's begin by looking at *the technique.* This is the skill, or command, of the fundamentals of your art. It is knowing what is good and what is bad; what works well and what doesn't work well. Blake has said, "No man can embrace true art until he has explored and cast out false art."

To throw in a few paragraphs to make a book contemporary, or to create a picture-book with the idea of producing a good seller ought not to be your intention. Your intention hopefully, is nothing less than obeying the will of the Lord and producing what the Holy Spirit guides you to do.

You can't make a book any better written by adding artwork, not can artwork improve the message. If it isn't in the words, it isn't there. You can take the most brilliant painting and reproduce it alongside an inferior piece of writing and the painting won't help it. In fact, both expressions will suffer.

Let's assume your unsubmitted manuscript or idea is in order and you have chosen to combine it visually with photography. You can acquire photographs by: a.) taking them yourself, b.) hiring a photographer to take them for you, or c.) buying photos from one of the many studios that have stock photographs on file for one-time use at specified rates.

You may also leave the entire matter in the hands of your publisher who will handle layout as well as the choice of photography. Your suggestions will be valuable, however, and here is where your forethought and preparation will show.

Technique, or skill, is necessary in selecting art. When you are examining a photograph or artwork, the question in your mind should not be, "Is it good?" Instead, ask, "What reaction does it evoke?" If the visual art makes a statement that is complete, it is usually superfluous to add to it.

Here is an example of what I mean. In my book, *City Psalms,* published by Moody Press, there is a poem entitled *Loneliness.* Printed on grey paper, it faces a photograph my husband took of a pigeon sitting on the ledge of the roof of our apartment building in New York City. The photograph has a lonely, desolate quality and I identified with it and wrote the words,

> *I knew loneliness*
> *before.*
> *Barren, scalding*
> *loneliness . . .*

which began the poem hidden in that arrested moment captured by the camera.

We could have selected a hundred other photographs for a poem about loneliness, but we used the one of the pigeon. It is a subtle, and yet compelling photograph that was not complete until a poem was added to it. Then it became complete. This is how you must choose your photographs and art. The photograph of the pigeon was in need of a story. Are your visuals obvious statements in themselves or are they pictures in need of a story?

If you are writing for magazines, you naturally study the magazine for its style and format, and you must do the same with visuals. There are certain styles and formats that each publication requires, and you must carefully observe these.

The publications using visuals as an integral means of expressing the message are: tracts, collections of verse, devotional books and, of course, children's books. The publisher's art department usually adds the artwork and the writer is involved only in the writing, except with children's books where artist and writer may work closely together.

Technique is not enough, however, in combining the written word and visual art. There are *the aesthetics* to consider.

There are certain principles of aesthetics and values that must not be violated.

If you are considering using illustrations with your writing, you must ask yourself more than once why visual experience is necessary in the work. When you have your illustrations in order, look for comparison and contrast of expression. Does the writing confront, whereas the illustrations merely encounter, or vice versa? What are you reflecting in the art and in the writing? Finally, does the message remain clear and precise throughout?

Because a photograph or picture is great, it doesn't mean it would arouse attention or move readers to action if combined with the written word. Often it detracts instead of adds to.

A picture isolates a mood or a feeling as words press into a mood or feeling. In Marshall McLuhan and Harley Parker's book, *Through the Vanishing Point,* they write, "The advantage of using poetry and art simultaneously is that one permits a journey inward, the other a journey outward to the appearance of things."

Now, let's look at the last and most important component of your work: *the message.*

The technique and the aesthetics are valuable, but without the message they have nothing to express.

The Christian author differs from the secular author in that his only motive is to convey the message of the Gospel of Christ. With this motive in the forefront of every word skittered across a page, the message is all important and more valuable than the writing and the art.

Examine the writing from the aspect of the message and ask: 1.) Is the message clear as it stands? 2.) Would visuals add an increased awareness of the message? 3.) Would the addition of visuals heighten the preception of the reader and direct his mind toward God?

Combining the Visual Arts with the Written Word

I recently bought a book filled with drawings, paintings, photographs, graphics with the written message in various quotes from the Bible and contemporary people in short paragraphs of pithy sayings. The book is striking, but the message is overpowered by the abundance of art. After reading the book, I am still not quite sure what was said.

The Christian writer and artist cannot forget that it is not the writing nor the art we wish to show off, but the *message.*

Photographs can be poetry in themselves, as they can be social commentaries in themselves. The idea of using art and writing together is not to overstate or demonstrate talent, but to make the message more dynamic and meaningful to the reader. The idea is to bring the reader closer to Jesus.

This does not mean that artistically we have any right to be shoddy, or less than the best. Far from it! We ought to be the finest craftsmen who ever put books together! We ought to be producing the finest literature and the most exciting art *because we have the most exciting message!*

To combine visual arts with written art you do not need to be an art director, nor do you need expert skill at the drawing board or in the darkroom. A good knowledge of visuals is valuable, however, and if you don't have it, find someone who does and collaborate.

If you have no training in art, your worst enemy is your own taste. One would hesitate to employ the services of a doctor who exclaims, "I don't know much about medicine, but I know what I like." The same applies to the writer with the attitude, "I don't know much about art, but I know what I like." What you like might not inspire anybody else.

With the necessary elements of technique, aesthetics and message formed to present a harmonious unit of words and art, we experience an expression which our visually-trained minds can receive gladly.

The Christian writer or artist is a person with a sense of active God expression, and one always finding in life something new and fresh to bring to others in the name of the Lord. Combining the visual arts with the written word is one idea. We need to explore every possibility.

22
Writing for Christian Radio

Jerry Rice
Director of Scriptwriting, WMBI

If you were to walk down the street and ask the next ten passers-by to describe Christian radio, their answers would probably range from, "What's Christian radio?" to, "Oh yeah, that's the station with the preachin' and the sacred music."

However, true Christian radio is more than exhortations by Brother Zeke or the endless repetition of great hymns of the church. The ministry of Christian radio is a precious, valuable means of proclaiming the Good News of Jesus Christ to a listening world.

It would be unfair as well as untrue to stereotype this ministry as one of only preaching and singing. For available to the Christian broadcaster today is a variety of ways to communicate a vital scriptural message.

One of these ways is dramatic programming. Once the backbone of secular radio's golden days, the radio drama has truly found a lasting home in Christian broadcasting. Its uses are unending . . . and so is its popularity.

Radio drama is the vehicle by which R.G. LeTourneau's life is portrayed in serial form . . . or it's an exciting 15-minute babysitter as children linger on every word of an adaptation of the popular Sugar Creek Gang series.

To many, the polished, well-paced dialogue of quality radio drama often sounds spontaneous, requiring little or no preparation. But there is indeed preparation . . . a great deal of it going into the central object of all radio drama—the script.

Just how important is a script in producing a dramatic radio program? Let's examine . . . .

To deliver his goods, a truck driver would need a road map to guide him through new and unfamiliar territory. In much the same way, the radio actor depends upon his script for direction in delivering his message. In both cases there are signals to obey, obstacles to avoid, and even speed limits to abide by.

If you have aspirations to become a script writer, you may want to consider the following questions and suggestions.

What makes a good dramatic script for Christian radio? Well, first and most important, the script's content must meet the objectives of the station or organization for which it was written. For example, the script objectives of the Moody Radio Network are fourfold: (1) to encourage believers; (2) to promote reliance on the Lord in every area of human experience; (3) to promote positive action in Christian experience; and (4) to evangelize. As is true with many Christian stations, the majority of the audience of the five-station Moody Radio Network consists of born-again believers. Therefore, the greater portion of dramatic thrust is on the first three points. However, all scripts should, at least indirectly, contain some evangelistic purpose. On some occasions, such as special seasonal programs, evangelism could play the major part in the objective.

It is particularly important in Christian radio that scripts do not end on a negative note. The script writer should strive to communicate positive action to the listener, offering spiritual approaches to life's problems. Never forget that people are looking for answers. It is the writer's job to supply those answers, using his creative efforts as a definite ministry.

Whether the script is original or an adaptation, the writer should always keep a specific goal clearly in mind, and then gear all his efforts towards attaining that goal.

A conscientious scriptwriter will ask himself questions on every line he has written . . . and then answer them. Questions such as: Does the script contain a discernible theme or message? What is it? . . . Is the plot realistic? . . . Are characterizations strong? . . . And are the motivations of the characters made clear and convincing?

Now, as to the mechanics of scriptwriting, the same basic requirements would apply to Christian and secular stations alike. Again, use the self-questioning approach. Try this check list in examining your script:

(1) How is the opening? Is it fast? Is interest aroused at once?

(2) Are the time, place, and characters clearly exposited in the opening scene?

(3) Is the over-all structure of the script good? Does it proceed swiftly and surely from inciting action, through well-planned minor climaxes, to a major climax?

(4) Are all characters in the script well drawn and properly identified at all times? Are any of the characters unnecessary?

(5) Are there any unproducible spots? Have you written in sound effects which are too complicated to produce? Do they add reality or confusion to the program?

(6) Are the sound effects and music called for in the script adequate? Is the script cluttered with unnecessary sound?

(7) Are all the scenes necessary?

(8) Are the scene transitions of the sort you want? Do they depict a change in location, attitude, or a short or long length of time?

(9) Are the scenes properly blocked so that it's clear at all times where the audience is in the scene, and where the characters are in relation to the audience?

(10) Are all entrances and exits covered with lines or sound? (A character cannot fade out unless he has either a line or a sound effect to fade on.)

(11) Is the action (both dramatic and physical) properly motivated?

(12) Are there lines which contain unconscious double meanings?

(13) Are there lines that are difficult for the actors to say? Is the dialogue realistic and consistent with the character image being created?

(14) Are some of the speeches too long?

(15) Is the script approximately the right length? If it's too long, what can be cut out? If it's too short, where can it be stretched most effectively?

Be especially selective in using sound effects in your script. Don't include every sound that might occur in a real life situation, but use only those sounds that will actually stimulate the listener into visualizing the scene. Determine if the sound serves a real purpose. Use it only if it helps to make something clear, adds realism or dramatic impact, or if the audience expects to hear it. Examine each sound in the light of these criteria. If it satisfies none of them, eliminate it. If there are omissions in the light of these needs, create a sound to fulfill the need.

So you see, there actually is a great deal of preparation in making a radio script and its resulting drama sound spontaneous. Writing for Christian radio is unique, and by no means an easy task. But it is an exciting and challenging ministry—one that bears its rewards in the changed lives of faithful listeners.

Part Eight
Markets

23
Adults

Adult publications run the gamut from those slanted for married people to denominational house organs. But even magazines reaching the same type of audience will each have a different emphasis.

Select the magazines you'd like to write for, then ask for some copies. Send stamps or money to cover postage. When you receive the samples, study them. Notice the different slants, writing style, lengths, etc. Then write your article and send it to the magazine you've specifically slanted it for. If it comes back, look over your targets again. It may be that another publication can use it, perhaps with minor changes. You'll soon find that you're selling more manuscripts than are being rejected.

ADULT BIBLE TEACHER (Church of the Nazarene), 6401 The Paseo, Kansas City, Mo. 64131. (M) Adult Christian education articles based on Uniform Sunday school lessons on methods, inspiration, lesson themes. Length : 250 to 1000 words. Pays $20 per 1000 words and up for articles on accepance; 10¢ per line and up for poetry. Send mss. to Department of Church Schools; Attention, John B. Nielson, Editor.

ADULT CLASS (American Baptist Board of Ed. and Publ.), Valley Forge, Pa. 19481. (Q) Sunday school quarterly for adults. Features a thorough treatment of the Uniform Lessons for Sunday church school. In each issue there are one or two articles, 1200-1600 words. Wants well-written articles dealing with subjects that provide inspiration or guidance, interesting information about Christian faith, history or practices, Bible background, Bible study, successful adult class methods and programs. Payment on acceptance, usually 1¢ per word.

AMERICA, 106 W. 56th St., New York, N.Y. 10019. Uses articles that report and comment on or interpret events and trends in the areas of politics, social and economic problems, letters and culture, as well as religion. Readership is well above average in education; interests are in weekly events of the world and domestic scene with special interest in religious affairs. Length: 1500 words. Pays on acceptance.

AMERICAN BIBLE SOCIETY RECORD (non-denominational), 1865 Broadway, New York, N.Y. 10023. (M—except the two months in which it is combined: May-June and July-August) Published for families. Payment is made upon acceptance.

APPLIED CHRISTIANITY, 7960 Crescent Ave., Buena Park, Calif. 90620. This digest-format magazine wants Biblically-based articles relating Christian truth to all areas of human life, thought and activity and showing Christian solutions to problems relating to economics, government, drugs, abortion, business, labor, law and order, etc. Length: 1200 words. Payment is $35 to $100 per article.

BAPTIST HERALD, 7308 Madison St., Forest Park, Ill. 60130. (M) Denominational periodical. Inspirational articles of general religious news. Pays small honorarium. Editor: Dr. R.J. Kerstan.

BAPTIST MEN'S JOURNAL, 1548 Poplar Ave., Memphis, Tenn. 38104. (Q) Features about outstanding Southern Baptist men; roles men play in making contributions of service to the Christian cause; depth articles on trends as they affect Southern Baptists. No fiction. Pays 2¾¢ per word, edited.

THE BAPTIST RECORD (Southern Baptist), Box 530, Jackson, Miss. 39205. (W) Newspaper format; state denominational paper. Published for the family. Needs brief feature articles on church methods, personalities and programs; on Baptist history, teachings and biography; on inspirational and devotional subjects. Can use human interest stories, puzzles, quizzes on a family page. No payment.

BETHANY GUIDE, The Christian Church, Box 179, St. Louis, Mo. 63166. (M) Articles in field of Christian education from 1250-1500 words should help readers better see how persons learn and grow. Pays 1¢ per word; sharp, glossy 8x10 photos at current commercial rate. No fiction, fillers, editorials, essays, meditations or verse.

BIBLICAL RECORDER, 301 Hillsborough St., Raleigh, N.C. 27603. (W) Seeks material for all age groups because it is published for the whole family. Most of the material is furnished gratis by correspondents and by publicity men of Baptists. Needs more human-interest stories with a moral and religious slant.

BUILDER, Mennonite Pub. House, Scottdale, Pa. 15683. (M) Uses articles slanted to leadership in local congregations. Materials, for most part, are solicited by the editorial staff. Pays up to 1½¢ a word.

THE CHAPLAIN, 122 Maryland Ave. N.E., Washington, D.C. 20002. Wants chaplaincy history, biography, rationale and program ideas. Length: 1200 words. Pays 2¢ per word.

CHILD EVANGELISM, Box 1156, Grand Rapids, Mich. 49501. (M) Uses each month one article of 1000-1500 words for the family. Features must deal constructively and scripturally with some family (emphasis on children) problem or project; for Reach and Teach dept. one how-to-do-it article of approx. 1200 words, as well as short features, for Sunday school superintendents, teachers, junior church, club and other children's leaders; one junior story, 1000-1200 words, problems of salvation or a step in Christian growth for lead character to solve biblically, not preachy but evangelical in tone; one primary story, 400-450 words, same requirements as junior; also puzzles, quizzes, short poems for both age levels. Pays 1¢ a word for first rights. All other material in CE magazine by assignment. *Write* for editorial guide.

THE CHRISTIAN (Christian Board of Publications), Box 179, St. Louis, Mo. 63166. (W) Meditations, about 500 words, $5; articles, 500-1500 words, $3-$10; short stories, 1350 maximum, $10; poems, 4-16 lines, $1-$5; cartoons, $3; photos, b/w glossies only, considered for covers, $3-$7.50. Subject matter: religion, theology, home, church, school, business or social life, historical events, seasonal topics. Humorous material suitable to a church journal is welcome. Payment at end of month of publication unless material is scheduled far ahead, then payment on acceptance.

THE CHRISTIAN ATHLETE, Traders National Bank Bldg., 1125 Grand Ave., Suite 812, Kansas City, Mo. 64106. The publication of the Fellowship of Christian Athletes, it "bridges the worlds of sports and faith." Aimed at high school, college and pro athletes and coaches. Uses personal profiles, articles, and features pertaining to sports; especially likes testimony and personal profiles of known and unknown athletes and coaches. Articles should have spiritual thrust. Query is good but not necessary. Good pictures a selling point for a mss. Length preferred: 1000 to 2500 words.

THE CHRISTIAN CENTURY, 407 S. Dearborn St., Chicago, Ill. 60605. (W) Articles wanted which help build the church as a free and voluntary community, especially promoting Christian unity and the ecumenical movement, offering a Christian commentary on national and international affairs. Payment is variable and made after publication.

Christian Educator's EDGE (Church of the Nazarene), 6401 The Paseo, Kansas City, Mo. 64131. (M) A magazine for all church school workers. Wants informative and inspirational articles of not more than 1000 words on all phases of Christian education and the local church. Very little poetry used. Pays 2¢ a word on acceptance.

CHRISTIAN HERALD, 27 E. 39th St., New York, N.Y. 10016. (M) Uses articles on all themes common to modern living, up to 2500 words. Many deal with social issues analyzed with relevance to Christian adults. Can use how-we-did-it suggestions on various phases of personal and group religious life. Prefers query and outline before seeing major articles. Pays $100 and up for full-length nonfiction; $10 and up for short pieces.

CHRISTIAN HERITAGE, 275 State St., Hackensack, N.J. 07602. Articles of about 2500 words should be related to its theme which is that *Christian Heritage* provides through its articles, international press reports, critical assessments of Protestant-Catholic relations and its Christ-centered evangelical message of hope for a world convulsed by unprecedented revolutionary changes.

CHRISTIAN JOURNAL (non-denominational), P.O. Box 2022, Oakland, Calif. 94604. For the whole family, especially for Bible believers; patriotic but not political, inspirational. Material furnished by ministers and/or public-spirited writers, gratis. Non-subscription, distributed to local (California) churches free of charge. Outside by mail 20¢ a copy. Non-profit.

CHRISTIANITY TODAY, 1014 Washington Bldg., Washington, D.C. 20005. (Bi-W) Articles, 1000-3500 words, on theological and other themes of evangelical Christian relevance. Scholarship must be unimpeachable. Pays $35-$100.

CHRISTIAN LIFE, Union Gospel Press, Box 6059, Cleveland, Ohio 44101. (Q) Evangelical and practical Christianity slanted for adults. Needs real-life articles and fiction between 750 and 1500 words. Payment 2¢ per word.

CHRISTIAN LIVING (Mennonite Publ. House), Scottdale, Pa. 15683. (M) Uses articles on the application of Christian principles to everyday living, especially in the family; particularly interested in articles that describe fresh approaches to old problems and that show evidence of research to back up the assertions in the articles; poems, pictures to illustrate articles. Pays up to 2¢ per word; poetry about $5 a poem.

THE CHRISTIAN MINISTRY, 407 S. Dearborn St., Chicago, Ill. 60605. (Bi-M) There is a theme for each issue; material on the themes stand the best chance of acceptance. It's best to first write the editor about the idea or subject you want to submit. Sermons, liturgical pieces, photos and prayers are always welcome. Tips about interesting developments or people are appreciated.

CHRISTIAN STANDARD, 8121 Hamilton Ave., Cincinnati, Ohio 45231. Uses articles of about 1600 words on Biblical doctrine, applied Bible exegesis, evangelism and stories of accomplishment in Christian life and service. Pays according to length and quality.

THE CHRISTIAN TEACHER, Box 550, Wheaton, Ill. 60187. (Q) A magazine for Christian school teachers, administrators, board members and parents. No set requirements. They publish content that has promise of being of worth to readers. Mss. bearing on the work of the Christian day school considered. Usually no payment. Of special interest to writers is an annual award for best children's book with a Christian message announced annually in May-June issue.

CHURCH ADMINISTRATION (Baptist), 127 Ninth Ave. N., Nashville, Tenn. 37254. (M) Wants articles, 750-1200 words, dealing with church programming, organization and staffing, administrative skills, church financing, church facilities, food service, communication, pastoral ministries and community needs. Pays 2½¢ per usable word for articles on acceptance. Desires mss. rather than queries.

THE CHURCH HERALD, 630 Myrtle St. N.W., Grand Rapids, Mich. 49504. This is the official magazine of the Reformed Church in America. Most of their readers are church-going families with a knowledge of basic biblical facts and truths. They are looking for articles that will help them interpret current issues in the light of God's revelation through Scripture and Jesus Christ. Articles can be from 800 to 2500 words with 1400 the preferred length. "Guidelines for Writers" as well as copies of the magazine are available on request.

CHURCHMAN, 1074 23rd. Ave. N., St. Petersburg, Fla. 33704. (M) Wants fine, thoughtful articles, mostly on the social scene (based on social gospel), or comments, from a Christian point of view, on current topics. Refreshingly international-minded. Does not pay.

THE CHURCH MUSICIAN, 127 Ninth Ave. N., Nashville, Tenn. 37234. Uses articles of about 1000 words concerning music in the local church, human interest stories, success stories, testimonials, "how-to-do-it" and inspirational articles. Pays ¼¢ per word.

CHURCH RECREATION (Baptist), 127 Ninth Ave. N., Nashville, Tenn. 37234. (Q) Ten percent free-lance. Wants articles of interest to all ages on drama, sports, crafts, camping, recreational leadership, retreats, hobbies, parties, banquets, fellowships, etc. Preferred length: 700-1400 words. Especially looks for a quality of personal experience, how the activity or program was organized and carried out and its results. Query suggested. In the area of fiction, skits and dramatic presentations suitable for presentation in churches are used. The latter are humorous and serious skits, dramatic productions with a Christian message. Same payment as for nonfiction. Buys photos with mss. b/w only; 5x7 or 8x10. Pays $2 or more per photo used. Buys first rights.

CO-LABORER (Official publication of the Woman's National Auxiliary Convention of Free Will Baptists), Box 1088, Nashville, Tenn. 37202. (M). Uses articles on missions and some inspirational or devotional materials slanted for women. Does not pay.

COLLOQUY, 1505 Race St., Rm. 807, Philadelphia, Pa. 19102. Uses essays on educational methods and philosophies, reports on local situations (usually experimental), reviews of books with educational significance. Wants fresh, non-scholarly style. Length should be 1000-2000 words. Pays $25 per page (800-1000 words).

THE CHURCH HERALD (Reformed Church in America), 630 Myrtle St. N.W., Grand Rapids, Mich. 49504. Seeks feature articles that deal with problems and issues the Christian faces in our present-day world; articles which show how Jesus Christ transforms individual lives and how Christian principles put to work in such lives can transform family life, society and government; research articles on significant facts or events relating to the Bible or Christian history; personality or biographical articles on well-known Christians of today. All should have evangelical slant without being preachy. Payment, 2¢ per word and up. Also can use children's stories on themes of present day interest with practical, moral and religious teaching; between 600-800 words at 2¢ per word and up.

CHURCH MANAGEMENT: The Clergy Journal, 115 N. Main St., Mount Holly, N.C. 28120. (M) Occasionally buys good articles on practical tried methods in finance, administration, psychology of leadership. Also buys articles of authority on modern church building. Slanted for Protestant clergymen. Pays from $5-$25 per article.

COMMONWEAL, 232 Madison Ave., New York, N.Y. 10016. Uses timely and thoughtful articles on issues of the day—political, socio-economic, cultural and religious. Length: 1000-3000 words. Payment on acceptance.

CONCERN, 475 Riverside Dr., New York N.Y. 10027. (M). Contributions come largely from solicited writers who interpret the program of United Presbyterian Women—a program of the United Presbyterian Church, U.S.A. Does not pay.

CONTACT (United Brethren Publication), 44 E. Franklin St., Room 302, Huntington, Ind. 46750. (W) Uses Christ-centered fiction, 1200-1500 words; how-to-do-it articles, 500-1500 words; devotional articles; "different" Bible quizzes; inspirational poems. Pays 2-3¢ for second rights and 3-4¢ for first rights and simultaneous submissions.

DAILY BLESSING, Oral Roberts Association, P.O. Box 2187, Tulsa, Okla. 74102. (Q) Uses meditations that are positive and uplifting in tone. Length: 50 characters per line, 27 lines including title and Scripture verse. Payment is $5-$15, depending upon editorial work involved. Inspiring articles conveying a blessing, up to 2000 words, $50 and up. Writers guide and sample copy sent upon request.

DAILY MEDITATION, P.O. Box 2710, San Antonio, Tex. 78206. Uses inspirational, self-improvement, nonsectarian religious articles showing the way to greater spiritual growth; experiences of God's mysterious ways; archaelogical discoveries pertaining or related to the ancient Maya; some poetry and fillers. No fiction. Length: articles—300, 750, 1200, 1650 words approx.; fillers—up to 350 words; poetry—4-12 lines most usuable, none over 20 lines. Be sure to give exact word count on each mss. Rates ½¢ to 1¢ per word on articles and fillers; 14¢ a line on poetry—paid on acceptance. Reports within 60 days. Two checking copies of issue using mss. sent to author upon publication.

DECISION Magazine, 1300 Harmon Pl., Minneapolis, Minn. 55403. Uses nonfiction articles, preferably testimonies or brief "as told to" accounts which convey what Christ has done. They encourage the writer to study the publication and notice the types of testimonies they use. Word length is approximately 1800 words. Uses devotional thoughts and short poetry for "The Quiet Heart" column. Five to eight-line verse poems, free verse, brief narrative, illustration for the "Editorial Feature" section. Fresh, quotable quips from known or unknown individuals, or devotional thoughts to be used as fillers. Payment is at discretion of editor upon publication.

ETERNITY, 1716 Spruce St., Philadelphia, Pa. 19103. (M) Can use well-written, organized articles on devotional, doctrinal and expository subjects slanted toward mature Christians who are interested in Bible study and the Biblical emphasis on contemporary developments. Most articles are written on special assignment. Some missionary articles with photos used. Articles should not exceed 2500 words. Pays 2¢-3¢ a word on acceptance.

EVANGEL (Free Methodist), Light and Life Press, Winona Lake, Ind. 46590. (W) Wants stories of 1800-2000 words, with strong characterization; plots based on contemporary problems, and recognition of changing world conditions as they affect the Christian life; religious emphasis without clumsiness or over-sentimentality. Short articles 400-800 words. Longer articles 1500 to 2000 words. Uses fillers of 200-500 words and some devotional poetry. Payment is 2¢ per word on acceptance, 25¢ per line for poetry.

EVANGELICAL BEACON (Evangelical Free Church of America), 1515 E. 66th St., Minneapolis, Minn. 55423. (Bi-W) Occasionally buys material from free-lancers, articles 1000-1500 words along devotional lines. Also photos, some poetry.

EVENT (The American Lutheran Church), 422 S. 5th St., Minneapolis, Minn. 55415. An issue-oriented magazine aimed at laity. Each issue focuses on single theme, like family, government, life and death, the city, church and military, etc. Nearly all manuscripts are solicited so inquiries are strongly recommended. Uses very little fiction, maybe one story a year. No fillers, quizzes, poetry, etc. Articles run about 1500 words and payment varies from $40-$1000. Interested in contacts with free-lance photographers. Sample copy available.

FAMILY DIGEST, Noll Plaza, Huntington, Ind. 46750. (M) Uses practical, humorous, inspirational, "confessional" concerned with family relations (husband-wife-children-teens-grandparents), family health, family finance, family spirituality, etc. Uses a topical format (parenthood, self-realization, nature, Redemption, home, marriage, vacation-travel, maturity, education, leisure, creativity, Incarnation) under commitment "Pathways to Joy: The Fun and Fulfillment of Family Life." Likes first-person or interview material. Uses very little verse or filler. Will accept reprints. Pays 4¢ a word and up, on acceptance.

FELLOWSHIP (Inter-faith), Box 271, Nyack, N.Y. 10960. (M) Nonfiction principally but some fiction, if related to central theme: creative, self-giving love in all situations, particularly of conflict and war. Prefers 500-1000 words; limit 2000 words. Real-life incidents of nonviolence in action especially desired; also analytical articles with religion implicit rather than explicit. No pay.

FLOODTIDE (interdenominational, missionary), Christian Literature Crusade, Inc., Box C, Fort Washington, Pa. 19034. (Q) Published for adults and for college-age young people. Uses articles featuring the power of the printed Gospel in lives, challenges to young people for full-time service and articles showing literature workers on the job in bookstore, book-mobile, publishing and other literature-related activities. Articles up to 750 words. Does not pay.

FREE WILL BAPTIST, Ayden N.C. 28513. (W) Uses one feature a week of general interest, personalities or unusual incidents. Should not be more than 2000 words.

FRIENDS JOURNAL (Society of Friends—Quakers), 152-A N. 15th St., Philadelphia, Pa. 19102. (Semi-M) Articles under 2000 words of fact or opinion on contemporary problems of social, ethical and religious concern. Occasional poetry. No payment.

GOSPEL CARRIER (Pentecostal Church of God of America), P.O. 850, Joplin, Mo. 64802. (W) Adult Sunday school take-home paper. Needs fiction and nonfiction with strong evangelical slant. Prefers 1500-2000 words. Payment on acceptance, ¼¢ per word. Uses poetry.

GUIDE (Seventh-day Adventist), Review and Herald Publ. Assn., Washington, D.C. 20012. (W) Wants true stories only. Should have positive approach, be dramatically written, inspiring readers to honesty, faithfulness, reverence, etc. Pays about 1½¢ per word.

GUIDEPOSTS, 3 West 29th St., New York, N.Y. 10001. An inspirational magazine written by and for people of all faiths. Uses short features up to 250 words as well as longer articles up to 1500 words, all true experiences with spiritual emphasis. Very few poems used.

HERALD OF HOLINESS (Church of the Nazarene), 6401 The Paseo, Kansas, City, Mo. 64131. (W) Articles from 600 to 800 words in length, written from a strictly evangelical point of view and dealing with practical problems of Christians in this present age. Payment is $8 per article, on publication. Send self-addressed envelope for return of unused mss.

HOME LIFE, 127 Ninth Ave. N., Nashville, Tenn. 37203. (M) Wants human interest material on actual Christian family experiences, fiction, poetry, all focusing on family life. Articles and fiction, 750-3000 words; poetry, 4-16 lines; pays 2½¢ per word on acceptance.

IDEALS, 11315 Watertown Plank Rd., Milwaukee, Wis. 53201. (Bi-M) Pays on publication $10 plus complimentary copy. Buys one-time rights. Reports in two weeks. Will send sample copy to a writer on request. Homespun variety, inspirational, patriotic, religious, seasonal, family, childhood or nostalgic. Do not send your only copy. Prose selections 1500 words or less.

INTERACTION (Lutheran), 3558 S. Jefferson Ave., St. Louis, Mo. 63118. (M) The purpose of *Interaction* is to bring before its readers theological, psychological and educational insights applicable to teaching in the church school. Articles up to 2000 words. Payment ranges from $10 to $50. They want a popular, readable style.

INTER-VIEW, P.O. Box 276, Houghton, N.Y. 14744. (Bi-A) This is a "scholarly journal of leadership development from the Christian perspective. They consider manuscripts, interviews and research from scholars, leaders and journalists in the field. Book reviews must be pertinent to leadership development. Some of this material will be published in the quarterly *Inter-View* bulletin. The journal accepts manuscripts in any language and summarizes them in English, Spanish and French. Sample copies $1.50; payment in complimentary copies.

KEY TO CHRISTIAN EDUCATION, 8121 Hamilton Ave., Cincinnati, Ohio 45231. (Q) Written for all Christian education leaders. Needs practical ideas on every facet of Christian education. One-page articles, 750 words, payment up to $20; two-page articles, 1500 words, payment up to $35. Tested ideas, 150 words, payment $5. Photos used $5 (more upon special arrangement with ed.). Not interested in Christian education theory. Strictly a "how-to" magazine for the Christian education worker.

Adults

LEARNING WITH (Lutheran), 2900 Queen Lane, Philadelphia, Pa. 19129. Appears in four age-level editions: young children, children, youth, adult. Looks for practical help for the Christian education teacher and administrator: approaches, trends, methods, philosophies, family and cross-generational events, "how-to" activities, stories for children, biblical background and insights, etc. Prefers articles describing actual situations. Maximum is 1500 words. Photos and/or art desired, but not necessary. Payment upon publication.

LIBERTY, 6840 Eastern Ave. N.W., Washington, D.C. 20012. Uses nonfiction, current events and historical (primarily former) dealing only with religious freedom and church-state separation in the U.S., Canada and throughout the world. Pays about $60 to $100 per article. Pictures accepted also: pays $7 black and white, more for color if used as color. Up to $150 for photo used on front cover.

LIGHT AND LIFE, Winona Lake, Ind. 46590. (Bi-W) Can use first-class poems (preferably with social service implications); devotional material; factual reports on civic and national affairs with implications for the church and its work. Does not pay.

THE LINK, 122 Maryland Ave. N.E., Washington, D.C. 20002. (M) For men and women in the armed forces. Wants young adult fiction that has 7 qualities: 1) it must be a story, have plot, struggle, conflict; 2) it must stir the emotions; 3) it must begin well; 4) it must have movement and wholeness; 5) its characters must be convincing; 6) it must be appropriate for the age group; 7) it must have a message. Length, 1500-2000 words; nonfiction: any subject that would be of interest primarily, but not exclusively, to Protestant military personnel and their families. Length, 800-1500 words. Can use pictures. Uses fillers, cartoons, puzzles and some short Christian poetry. Pays 1¢-1½¢ per word on acceptance.

LIVE, Gospel Publishing House, 1445 Boonville Ave., Springfield, Mo. 65802. (W) Fiction presenting believable characters working out their problems according to biblical principles, character building without being preachy, 1200-1800 words. Articles with reader appeal presented realistically, up to 1000 words. Biography or missionary material using fiction techniques. Historical, scientific or nature material with a spiritual lesson. Brief fillers, purposeful, usually containing an anecdote with strong evangelical emphasis. Up to 500 words. Pays ½¢-1¢ per word on acceptance.

THE LIVING CHURCH, 407 E. Michigan St., Milwaukee, Wis. 53202. (W) All material is written primarily for Episcopalians by Episcopalians who are experts in the fields on which they write. News is provided by regular correspondents and news sources almost entirely. Articles are on subjects of current interest to church people and devotional subjects on a high level. Little verse is accepted and none paid for. Article length 500-1000 words. Small honorarium for articles, paid on demand.

THE LOOKOUT, Seamen's Church Institute of New York, 15 State St., New York, N.Y. 10004. The basic purpose of the publication is to engender and sustain interest in the work of the Institute and to encourage monetary gifts in support of its philanthropic work among seamen. Emphasis is on the merchant marine: pleasure yachting, power boats, commercial or pleasure fishing, passenger vessels. Buys free-lance marine-oriented articles (on the old and new, oddities, adventure, factual accounts, unexplained phenomena) of around 200 to 1000 words (together with art) for up to $40. Does not use fiction. Buys small amount of short verse, paying $5. Does not use technical pieces; most readers are lay-persons, not seafarers. Buys vertical format b/w (no color) cover photos on sea-related subjects, paying $20, lesser amounts for miscellaneous photos used elsewhere in the book. Pays on publication. Prefers queries. Sample copies provided on request.

THE LOOKOUT (Standard Publ. Co.), 8121 Hamilton Ave., Cincinnati, Ohio 45231. (W) Needs short stories of 1000-1200 words, and serials of 4-8 installments of 1200 words each. Also needs articles of 1000-1200 words. Chiefly methods or news-type articles on phases of educational work of the local undenominational church on dealing with personal or family problems of Christian life or work. Will buy glossy photos, 8x-10, human interest or scenics. Pays up to $35 for short stories, up to $35 a chapter for serials, up to $25 for articles, up to $10 for photos.

LORENZ PUBLISHING CO., Dayton, Ohio 45401. Publishes subscription choir magazines of anthems for every Sunday of the year. Wants anthem lyrics of 2-3 stanzas. Also publishes short articles (not more than 500 words) of interest to choirs and choir directors. Prices are in line with other buyers.

THE LUTHERAN, 2900 Queen Lane, Philadelphia, Pa. 19129. Uses articles, 1500 word maximum, on church at work, personal religious life, great Christian personalities. Photos always helpful. Address queries to Features Editor. Pays about 5¢ per word on acceptance.

THE LUTHERAN STANDARD, 426 S. 5th St., Minneapolis, Minn. 55415. Uses articles relating faith to daily living and to social problems. Examples of people or congregations (especially Lutherans) who live out their faith. Length: 600-1200 words.

MARRIAGE, St. Meinrad, Ind. 47577. Uses 4 different types of articles. (1) Informative and inspirational articles on all aspects of marriage, especially husband and wife relationship. Length, 2000-2500 words. (2) Personal essays relating dramatic or amusing incidents that point up the human side of marriage. Up to 1500 words. (3) Profiles of outstanding couple or couples whose story will be of interest for some special reason and profiles of individuals who contribute to the betterment of marriage. Length, 1500-2000 words. (4) Interviews with authorities in the fields of marriage (on current problems and new developments). Length: up to 2000 words. Pays 5¢ per word. Photos purchased with mss., b/w glossies or color transparencies. Pays $17.50, half-page; $35, full-page. Requires model releases.

MATURE YEARS (Methodist), 201 Eighth Ave. S., Nashville, Tenn. 37203. (Q) Stories dealing with problems and interests of older adults and shut-ins; poetry (not longer than 14 lines). Pays 2¢ per word for prose and 50¢ a line for poetry.

MENNONITE BRETHREN HERALD, 159 Henderson Hwy., Winnipeg 5, Man., Canada. (W) Published for the whole family. Idea articles, interpreting biblical teaching on the Christian life into real life situations within the family and in the community. Best length 1500-2500 words. Youth (15-21 years) slanted stories and articles. Should make a strong appeal to witnessing and to living a truly changed life. Best length 1000 to 1500 words. Payment 14¢ per column inch. Pictures with articles welcomed.

MISSIONARY BAPTIST SEARCHLIGHT, Box 663, Little Rock, Ark. 72203. (Bi-M) A newspaper (religious). News is compiled in editorial office. No rate of pay, but will use contributions if they are suitable.

MOODY MONTHLY, 820 N. LaSalle, Chicago, Ill. 60610. (M) Uses personal experience articles, devotionals (factual and anecdotal development), solid treatment of contemporary problems, seasonals, non-promotional features on Christian organizations or works, Christian education or other church-related articles. They should be warm, evangelical and clearly relevant to the daily life of a Christian. Length should be 1700-2200. Payment is 3¢ a word.

MUSIC MINISTRY, United Methodist Publ. Hse., 201 Eighth Ave. S., Nashville, Tenn. 37202. (M) Magazine is intended for all persons in positions of music leadership in church and church school. Articles dealing with any facet of the ministry of music in the life of the church are invited. Length: 1200-1800 words. Pays about 2¢ a word. Limited amount of appropriate fiction considered.

NEW WORLD OUTLOOK, 475 Riverside Dr., Room 1328, New York, N.Y. 10027. It is the award-winning monthly magazine of the United Methodist and United Presbyterian churches. Articles focus on missional issues around the world and in the United States and what Christians are doing to meet these issues and to present a living faith relevant to today's world. Length: 1500-2000 words. Pays on publication from $40 to $100 depending on length. Black and white glossies are desirable.

THE PENTECOSTAL EVANGEL (Official organ of the Assemblies of God), 1445 Boonville Ave., Springfield, Mo. 65802. (W) Wants true stories of conversions, bodily healing through faith in Christ, any remarkable answer to prayer. Uses fiction for Mother's Day, Father's Day, Thanksgiving, Christmas. Also wants devotional articles, Bible studies, articles telling how to be saved, 650-750 words, articles on Christian living, 800-1000 words; fillers, various lengths. Pays 1¢ and up per word on publication for first rights. Uses second rights material also.

THE PENTECOSTAL MESSENGER (Pentecostal Church of God of America), P.O. Box 850, Joplin, Mo. 64801. Requires material primarily for adults and young people. Some material for junior age level is used. Needs Bible-based sermons conforming to fundamental teaching; human interest articles with spiritual relevance; and inspirational articles or poems with seasonal effect.

THE PENTECOSTAL TESTIMONY (Pentecostal Assemblies of Canada), 10 Overlea Blvd., Toronto 17, Ont., Canada. (M) Needs 1000-word, salvation-message articles with strong evangelistic appeal. Can use articles on Pentecostal doctrine. Should be of general interest, clear, sound and scriptural. True stories of soul winning, outstanding conversions and answers to prayer written in first person. Uses stories, 400-500 words, on junior age level with the moral built into the story. Authentic pictures illustrating feature articles welcome; payment $2.50 or more. Pays 50¢ per 100 words for manuscripts. Poems, minimum payment $2.50. Payment made upon publication.

POWER FOR LIVING, Scripture Press Publications, Inc., Wheaton, Ill. 60187. (W) Sunday school paper for adults. Wants a variety of nonfiction that will help the reader realize that it is Christ who supplies the power for joyous living: profiles of colorful Christians whose achievements make them article material; first-person stories of how God has helped individuals to triumph in different circumstances; adventures—missionary and otherwise. Wants adult fiction that's true to life, gives unpreachy Christian impact. Pays up to 4¢ a word. Ask for "Tips to the Writer" packet.

THE PRESBYTERIAN RECORD, 50 Wynford Dr., Don Mills, Ont. M3C 1J7, Canada. Uses nonfiction: inspirational, factual, informative, general interest of interest to Canadian Presbyterians. Includes material for all ages. Length: 1500 words, short features 400 to 800 words. Pays $10 to $25.

PRESBYTERIAN SURVEY (Presbyterian Church of United States), 341 Ponce de Leon Ave. N.E., Atlanta, Ga. 30308. (M) Buys first rights to articles dealing with current issues before the church. Mss. should be 1200-1800 words in length and submitted with a return envelope. Allow 6 weeks for evaluation.

QUAKER LIFE (Friends United Meeting), Friends Central Offices, 101 Quaker Hill Dr., Richmond, Ind. 47374. (M) Carries articles of inspiration and information for the Society of Friends and the larger fellowship of the church. Does not pay.

RELIGION AND SOCIETY, Box 244, Stillwater, Minn. 55082. Articles must focus on a contemporary problem in such a way that the message is timeless. Must be with the background of academic knowledge, but must also be directed to laymen. Needs good literature that is historically informed. Not interested in "love" articles or mental health. Interested in classical economics as a basis of social reform. Advances the limitations of government rather than the efficacy of government. Pays in additional copies of journal in which article appears.

REVIEW AND EXPOSITOR, 2825 Lexington Rd., Louisville, Ky. 40206. (Q) Articles of moderate length on church-related themes. Well-documented and directed mainly to pastors and Christian workers with college degrees or advanced study. Highly-technical reports of biblical studies not used. No payment.

THE REVIEW OF BOOKS AND RELIGION, Box 2, Belmont, Vermont 05730. Uses book reviews and articles based on books. Only recent books are of interest to the editorial staff. An occasional longer review article is used; but in all cases a query should first be addressed to the editor. Unsolicited book reviews are discouraged. However, the editor likes to have interested persons offer to do reviews in religion and adjacent fields such as psychology, sociology, literature, etc. The reviewer keeps the book reviewed.

THE SABBATH RECORDER, Seventh Day Baptist Bldg., 510 Watchung Ave., Plainfield, N.J. 07060. (W) Primarily a denominational organ, 16-page weekly. (Special issues in color 3 times per year.) Normally contains missions, Christian education and women's department. Does not pay.

SCIENCE OF MIND Magazine, 3251 West Sixth St., Los Angeles, Calif. 90020. Desires articles uniting science, philosophy and religion. Also personal experience articles relating spiritual healing. All material must have spiritual import. Length: 1500-2400 words. Pays 1½¢ per word.

SCOPE, 422 S. Fifth St., Minneapolis, Minn. 55415. (M) Prefers brief timely and relevant articles and illustrative stories with definite Christian orientation slanted for average church woman. Glossy photos and filler material welcome. Payment varies.

SEEK, 8121 Hamilton Ave., Cincinnati, Ohio 45231. (W) Needs articles of personal interest and inspiration, controversial subject matter and timely issues of religious, ethical or moral nature, 800 to 1200 words. Pays approx. 2¢ a word.

SIGNS OF THE TIMES, 1350 Villa, Mountain View, Calif. 94040. Uses short devotional articles, about 1800 words, showing the meaning of the gospel in personal and and family life. Freshness of style and relevance to today's living are important. Pays $40 to $70.

SOCIAL JUSTICE REVIEW, 3835 Westminster Pl., St. Louis, Mo. 63108. Uses articles of research, editorial and review; 2000-4000 words at $3 per column. No fiction.

SPIRITUAL LIFE, 2131 Lincoln Rd. N.E., Washington, D.C. 20002. Serious articles about man's encounter with God in the 20th century. Language of articles should be college level. Technical terminology, if used, should be clearly explained. Material should be presented in a positive manner. Sentimental articles or those dealing with specific devotional practices not accepted. Articles should avoid the "popular" sentimental approach to religion and concentrate on a more intellectual approach. Sample copy of the magazine is sent upon request. Length: 4000 words. Pays $50 and up, depending on quality and length.

STANDARD, 6401 The Paseo, Kansas City, Mo. 64131. (W) Distributed free through the Sunday schools of the Church of the Nazarene. Uses stories which show young people (older college or above) and adults solving true-to-life situations through application of Christian principles. Prefers 2500 words. Serials of not more than three parts, each part approx. 2500 words. Avoid preachiness. Secure free folder, "Suggestions to Contributors" to learn taboos. Free sample copy. Pays 2¢ a word on acceptance.

SUCCESS (Baptist), 12100 W. Sixth Ave., Denver, Colo. 80215. (Q) This is a Christian Education magazine and therefore solicits nonfiction articles on subjects of general Christian Education interest and information. The articles may fit specific departments such as Preschool, Elementary, Youth or Adult; or may be slanted to all departments in general. Length, 500-2500 words. Payment, 1¢ to 3¢ per word, based on value of article to publication and amount of editing required. No query necessary. Photos directly connected with the article are welcome. Good sharp jumbo snapshots or Polaroid pictures are acceptable. Payment for photos, $1 to $10. Free sample copy and information sheet sent to writers upon request.

SUNDAY DIGEST, David C. Cook Publ. Co., 850 N. Grove, Elgin, Ill. 60120. (W) Uses articles of the following types (listed in order of frequency): personal experience, personality profile, self-improvement, fiction, missionary, church and Bible history. Interested in reprints. Word length is up to 2000 words. Pays up to 5¢ a word on acceptance.

SUNDAY SCHOOL COUNSELOR (National Sunday school organ of the Assemblies of God), 1445 Boonville Ave., Springfield, Mo. 65802. (M) This publication is addressed to Sunday school leaders, teachers and workers. Needs articles conveying inspiration and information on all phases of Sunday school work, with heavy emphasis on the how-to-do-it approach. News, feature and photo stories with a Sunday school slant are included occasionally. Length averages 1000 words. Pays up to 2¢ per word on acceptance. "Samplers," a monthly feature, carries practical suggestions for each age level. Length, 250 words; pays up to $7 for ideas.

THE SUNDAY SCHOOL TIMES AND GOSPEL HERALD, Union Gospel Press, Box 6059, Cleveland, Ohio 44101. Semi-monthly family magazine. Uses Bible studies and devotionals up to 1000 words. Real-life fiction stories, 500-1500 words. Pays 2¢ per word.

TEACH, Box 1591, Glendale, Calif. 91209. (Q) Basically a "how-to" magazine for Sunday school leaders and workers, to inform, inspire and train. Most articles done by assignment. If a contributor is interested in doing a longer article, he should query first. "Tips for Teach," a main section of the magazine, is wide open to free-lance contributions and pays $5 for every idea used. Ideas submitted should be those used by the contributor himself in Sunday school work, or those he has seen work from a first-hand viewpoint. Welcomes submissions for "Kid Stuff" which are humorous, thought-provoking or startling statements by children and young people. Originality, freshness—in a word, reality—are of prime importance. Pays $2 each for each contribution used. Pays 2¢ to 4¢ a word for articles, 25¢ to 50¢ a line for poetry. Prefers light verse, 4-8 lines, which carries out purpose of magazine.

THESE TIMES (Seventh Day Adventist), Box 59, Nashville, Tenn. 37202. (M) Inspirational, religious, non-doctrinal articles. No fiction. Some religious poetry. Pays 6¢ per word.

THOUGHT, 441 E. Fordham Rd., Bronx, N.Y. 10458. Scholarly but not excessively technical articles on all fields of learning and culture dealing with questions having permanent value and contemporaneous interest. Length: 5000-10,000 words. No pay except reprints.

TODAY (Harvest Publications and Gospel Light Publications), 1233 Central, Evanston, Ill. 60201. (W) Interview articles, 800-1200 words; true adventure, 800-1200 words; short fiction, 1400-1500 words; anecdotes, 400 words; current-interest topical articles, 800-1200 words; photo stories of all above categories, with half the wordage. Keep the spiritual point clear but smoothly integrated. Seasonal material should be in at least nine months before publication date. Pays 4¢ per word and up (month after acceptance), depending on significance of subject, quality of writing, etc. Photos, $2-$6 each. Query advisable. Complete packet of samples, suggestions and specifications for *Today* and other take-home papers, 50¢.

TODAY'S CHRISTIAN MOTHER (Standard Publishing), 8121 Hamilton Ave., Cincinnati, Ohio, 45231. Short, pertinent articles, 600-1000 words, showing the problems and pleasures of Christian child training in the home. Payment varies, depending on quality and length. No query necessary.

TOGETHER (general magazine of the United Methodist Church), 1661 N. Northwest Highway, Park Ridge, Ill. 60068. Is looking for vital, challenging material about individual belief, church, family and citizenship in the community, nation, world. Its goals are to help readers in their personal growth in the Christian faith, to report on denominational and ecumenical affairs and to present the contemporary world in Christian perspective. Prefers fast-moving anecdotal style. Approach does not include devotional material or preachments. Major features from 2000 to 3000 words, shorter features 750 to 1500 words. Ecumenical material should have some United Methodist aspect. Poems and cartoons used as fillers. Payment is on acceptance, varies according to quality, originality and timeliness.

THE TEXAS METHODIST, P.O. Box 1076, Dallas, Tex. 75221. Uses features of 750 words on persons putting Christianity to work in their daily lives. Pays 3¢ a word.

20th CENTURY CHRISTIAN, 2809 Granny White Pike, Nashville, Tenn. 37204. (M) Presents New Testament Christianity in this present age. All materials must be scrutinized in view of Bible teachings. Also *Power for Today,* daily devotional guide for the family. Does not pay.

THE UNION SIGNAL, 1730 Chicago Ave., Evanston, Ill. 60201. Editorials staff written, features written by medical men, research people, experts in the field of narcotic research. Does not pay. Published by the WCTU.

THE UNITED CHURCH OBSERVER, 85 St. Clair Ave. E., Toronto 7, Ont., Can. (M) Human interest stories of the church at work (through organizations and/or individuals) in Canada and overseas. Personal experience articles if they describe something exciting or of significance to Canadians. Articles no longer than 2000 words. Photo illustrations. Payment according to merit.

UNITED EVANGELICAL (Official publication of the Evangelical Congregational denomination), 100 W. Park Ave., Myerstown, Pa. 17067. (Bi-W) For all ages. Needs short stories and articles suitable for home reading; evangelical devotional articles and how-to-do-its for the average church, Sunday school and other church organizations. Does not pay.

UNITED EVANGELICAL ACTION, Box 28, Wheaton, Ill. 60187. (Q) Desires articles 1800-2000 words on social and theological issues with a distinct evangelical orientation. Payment varies on acceptance. Voice of the National Association of Evangelicals.

UNITY Magazine, Unity Village, Mo. 64063. Uses metaphysical and inspirational articles about 1500 words. No fiction. Pays 2¢ a word and up, on acceptance.

THE UPPER ROOM, 1908 Grand Ave., Nashville, Tenn. 37203. (Bi-M) Meditations are purely devotional. They must be world-wide and non-sectarian, presenting in positive terms the merits of the Gospel of Christ in all its fullness and power. A meditation should include a good pointed story. It should not be so familiar that it is threadbare. The meditation should develop one idea only. The maximum of 250 words includes Bible text, body, prayer and thought for the day which must not be poetry. Meditations should be received at least ten months in advance of publication date. If quoting a scientific fact or statistic, give source. Payment is $5. Leaflet on writing meditations and topics free on request.

WORLD VISION MAGAZINE, 919 Huntington Dr., Monrovia, Calif. 91016. Presents a wide range of facts and authoritative opinion relating to developments, issues and problems of Christian missions. No fiction or poetry. Most articles are assigned to experienced missionary personnel and renowned Christian leaders, but occasionally free-lance articles with missionary significance and reporting excellence are purchased. Articles should be no longer than 1200 words. Pays approximately 3¢ per word; $5 for good photos.

YOUR CHURCH Magazine, 198 Allendale Rd., King of Prussia, Pa. 19406. The major subjects covered in *Your Church* are: church architecture and design; audio-visual equipment and material; art, symbolism and book reviews; church equipment and administration; church finances; worship, church school and special ministries. Manuscripts should be 10 to 12 typewritten, double-spaced pages. Also, any illustration, black and white or color 8x10 glossy photos, 4x5 color transparencies or artwork, will be considered to accompany publication of the manuscript. If a mss. is accepted the author will be contacted concerning honorarium, which is payable upon publication.

YOUTH LEADER (American Baptist Board of Ed. and Publ.), Valley Forge, Pa. 19481. Articles 750-1500 words on teen-age psychology from the Christian viewpoint; successful teen-age church school classes and youth programs; guidance for adult counselors; teaching methods in youth classes; suggestions to leaders; philosophy of ministry with youth.

CHRISTIAN LIFE, Gundersen Dr. and Schmale Rd., Wheaton, Ill. 60187. (M) Slanted for alert Christians, this magazine is looking for articles which show how God is working in the world today—through the lives of individual Christians, organizations, missions. Uses trend articles (2,500-3,000 words) which provide evidence of significance and development of an idea, event, or person's impact on society and the meaning of that impact for the reader; inspirational and devotional articles (1,500-2,500 words); true adventure articles (2,000 to 2,500 words) which use short story techniques; short stories up to 2,500 words; personality profiles (up to 2,500 words) and general features. Photos should accompany articles when possible. Payment is up to $175 on publication.

CHRISTIAN BOOKSELLER, Gundersen Dr. and Schmale Rd., Wheaton, Ill. 60187 (M) This trade magazine, serving religious bookstores and general bookstores with religious book departments, needs articles which develop, in depth, business techniques for Christian bookstores. Reports on industry trends and unusual bookstores also needed. Feature articles are 1,000 to 1,500 words in length. Payment: 3-5¢ per word on publication. Also uses articles about personal training and managerial/administration how-to articles.

24
Roman Catholic Adults

COLUMBIA, P.O. Drawer 1670, New Haven, Conn. 06507. Geared to a general Catholic audience, but caters particularly to the members of the Knights of Columbus and their families. Fact articles 1000 to 3000 words. Should be directed to the Catholic laymen and family and deal with current events, social problems, Catholic apostolic activities, education, rearing a family, literature, science, arts, sports and leisure. Payment ranges from $100 to $300. 8 x 10 glossy photos are required for illustration. Articles without ample illustrative material are not accepted. Fiction up to 3000 words. Should be written from a thoroughly Christian viewpoint. Payment up to $300. Short humor or satire features, about 1000 words. Payment $100. Photo stories used with the same theme as fact articles. Payment, $10 per photo and 10¢ a word. Covers should have simple humor theme or special occasion illustrations such as Christmas, Easter, Columbus Day. Payment, $600. Artist should submit preliminary color sketch. Cartoons must show pungent, wordless humor. Payment, $25. Pays on acceptance. It accepts only original, exclusive material.

THE COMPANION OF ST. FRANCIS AND ST. AN-
THONY, 15 Chestnut Park Rd., Toronto, Ont., Can.
M4W 1W5. Wants articles about live, modern topics. They
should be of fairly wide interest to Canadians as well as to U.S.
citizens. Length: 1200-1500 words. Uses wholesome, not
preachy fiction of 1200-1500 words. Photos should be b/w, 5x7
if possible. Pays 2¢ per word, extra for photos used. For the
family.

FRANCISCAN MESSAGE, Pulaski, Wis. 54167. A
magazine of general interest but preferably based on solid
Catholic theology and the Franciscan spirit. Prefers length to
be 900-1500 words.

THE LAMP, Graymoor, Garrison, New York 10524. Uses
material, 1500-2000 words, on grassroots ecumenism,
especially local activities which promote Christian unity. Pays
about $50 for a mss.

THE LITTLE FLOWER MAGAZINE, P.O. Box 5280, San
Antonio, Tex. 78201. Wants tightly-written material on very,
very specific religious topics e.g. the origin of the Psalms in
community prayer; Gnostic influences on Paul and its
relevance today when the young are taken up with mysticism;
Teresa of Avila on meditation; no general articles on religion
or how nice the Bible is; little interest in the "how I found God"
piece unless it is remarkably well written or unusual; no "letters
to" articles. Material must be simplified for older, uneducated
readership. Material must be factual; don't be afraid to sum-
marize good scriptural commentary material, good
biographies of religious figures of the past or present; give
credit to your source in a brief mention (no footnotes).
Length:1250 words. Most material is donated; 1¢ a word.

MARIAN HELPERS BULLETIN, Eden Hill, Stockbridge,
Mass. 01262. Articles and photos of general interest, 300-1200
words, on devotional, spiritual, moral and social topics with a
positive and practical emphasis. Payment varies and is made
upon acceptance.

MESSENGER OF THE SACRED HEART, Box 100, Station G, Toronto 8, Ont., Can. (M) Needs articles and short stories to 2000 words which reflect the problems North American Catholics meet in their daily lives. Pays 2¢ a word and up. For adults.

NEW CATHOLIC WORLD, 1865 Broadway, New York, N.Y. 10458. Uses fiction, nonfiction and poetry based on the themes of each issue. Should be 2000 words, 10 pages double-spaced. Payment depends on length of article or poem. For adults.

THE NORTH AMERICAN VOICE OF FATIMA, 1023 Swan Rd., Youngstown, N.Y. 14174. Uses Marian articles and short stories, 1000 words. Pays 1¢ per word. For adults.

OUR FAMILY, Box 249, Dept. E, Battleford, Sask., Can. SOMOEO, Wants articles, 1000-3500 words, that deal with practical topics that concern people in their everyday lives —problems of home, youth, marriage, church, community, national and international affairs. Fiction, 1500-3000 words, that reflects the lives, problems and preoccupations of the reading audience. When possible, photos should be submitted with articles (or their availability noted). Pays $5 and up per photo. Payment for articles and fiction is 1¢ to 2¢ a word and up, on acceptance. A writer's guide is available upon request. For adults.

OUR LADY OF THE SNOWS, 15 S. 59th St., Belleville, Ill. 62223. Wants short articles, 200-500 words, that are inspiring and encouraging; articles which show by example how religion benefits readers; articles about the Blessed Virgin Mary, especially those which show how devotion to her benefits individual lives. Pays 10¢ per word; $5 for photos. For adults.

OUR SUNDAY VISITOR, Noll Plaza, Huntington, Ind. 46750. Uses general interest features, 1000 words, particularly those of interest to a Roman Catholic audience. Also 4-color photo features. Pays $75 and up. For teen-agers up.

PASTORAL LIFE MAGAZINE, St. Paul Monastery, Canfield, Ohio 44406. *Pastoral Life,* for clergymen, is a professional review, principally designed to focus attention on the current problems, needs, issues and all important activities related to all phases of pastoral work and life. It avoids merely academic treatment on abstract and too controversial subjects. Pays minimum of 2¢ per word.

PREACHING TODAY, 3015 4th St. N.E., Washington, D.C. 20017. Uses articles on preaching and related acts and sciences. Length: 2000 words. For adults.

QUEEN OF ALL HEARTS Magazine, 40 S. Saxon Ave., Bay Shore, L.I., New York 11706. (Bi-M) Uses articles, stories, poems about Mary, the mother of God. Length: 1200 words. Pays about 3¢ a word for articles and stories; does not pay for poetry.

REVIEW FOR RELIGIOUS, 539 N. Grand, St. Louis, Mo. 63103. (Bi-M) Published for men and women of the Roman Catholic church. Articles, on any subject of interest to this group, are from 1000 to 10,000 words in length. Pays $5 per printed page. Fiction also used, with same payment. Poetry, 50¢ per line.

SANDAL PRINTS, 1820 Mt. Elliott Ave., Detroit, Mich. 48207. Almost totally staff written. Queries accepted for articles about the work the Capuchins are doing in any apostolic field in the world. The preference is for the work of the midwest Capuchins. Pictures must accompany the article (unless something can be worked out to the contrary). Length 2000-3000 words. Payment varies.

THE SIGN, Monastery Place, Union City, N.J. 07087. (M) Needs articles focusing primarily on renewal within the church; profiles on people who dramatically exemplify what it means to be a Christian; fiction, articles emphasizing positive values in contemporary art and literature, politics and economics, science and technology. Pays $150-$400 on acceptance. Adult.

SISTERS TODAY, St. John's Abbey, Collegeville, Minn. 56321. Uses in-depth studies of religious life in the Catholic Church today; the role of women; religion in the Church and in the world; the theology and practice of the evangelical vows of poverty, chastity and obedience; religious community life today, its promises and problems; pertinent Biblical commentaries; the analysis of spiritual and psychological growth; development and deepening of personal and communal prayer life. No poetry. Length: 3000-5000 words. Pays $5 per printed page upon publication. Free-lance writers who have not had solid theological preparation and background as well as those who have had little or no experience of organized religious life today are *not* encouraged to submit manuscripts.

OUR SUNDAY VISITOR, Noll Plaza, Huntington, Ind. 46750. (W) Uses feature and human interest articles, 1000 words, with orientation to a Roman Catholic audience. Pays up to $100. All ages.

TODAY'S CATHOLIC TEACHER, 38 W. 5th St., Dayton, Ohio 45402. Wants articles on educational theory and practice, particularly as related to Catholic and other nonpublic schools. Most articles are written on assignment but occasionally a free-lance article is purchased. Length: 1200 words. Pays $20 to $75.

TRIUMPH, 278 Broadview Ave., Warrenton, Va. 22186. Wants in-depth analysis of political, theological and philosophical issues from an orthodox Catholic standpoint. Length: 3000 words. Pays 2½¢ per word. For adults.

WORKING FOR BOYS, 601 Winchester St., Newton Highlands, Mass. 02161. Address all mss. to Brother Jason, CFX, 800 Clapboardtree St., Westwood, Ma. 02090. For the family. Uses seasonal material, also factual and historical. Fiction, not necessarily religious. Quizzes and poetry. Length: 1000 words. Pays 3¢ a word, 25¢ per line for seasonal poems of not more than 12 lines long.

25
Young Adults

(ages 17-25)

What are high school seniors and college-age young people like? Very much like adults without the maturity experience brings. As you write for them, use their problems. These young people think clearly and well, without the prejudices and preconceived ideas which many adults have. Give them something to think about, something to live for.

CAMPUS AMBASSADOR MAGAZINE (CAM), 1445 Boonville Ave., Springfield, Mo. 65802. Articles addressing current or basic campus situations from a biblical viewpoint. The readers are almost all collegians so all material, whether inspirational or apologetic, must fit the university scene. Length is 900-1200 words. Payment is 1¢ per word.

COMPANION, P.O. Box 833, Harrisonburg, Va. 22801. (W) Uses short stories of 1000-1500 words, serials of two or more installments and character-building biographies, personal experiences and historical fiction. The youth column uses articles and essays up to 800 words on the problems and concerns of youth with direct spiritual emphasis; must be lively and interesting. Sunday Evening Program Planning Guide needs individual or monthly program outlines, topics, sermon suggestions and related features. Short articles clarifying scientific issues from a biblical perspective, from 200-500 words, are used in the Science and the Scriptures column. Also uses miscellaneous features from 200-500 words and meditations of 100-200 words. Poetry on devotional or spiritual themes should be about 20-30 lines. Pays 1¢ per word for first rights for stories and nonfiction; meditations, $1.50; Sunday evening program outlines up to $3.00 per outline; poetry up to 10¢ per line for first rights. All payment lower for second rights. Payment is made on acceptance.

COURIER, 1228 W. Lincoln Ave., Milwaukee, Wis. 53215. (M) Interdenominational publication is especially interested in testimonies of approx. 3500 words of college-age young people. Also articles that have campus interest, with a direct approach to God and Jesus Christ as Savior. Also uses articles of interest to career-age young people not in college.

FREEWAY, 1825 College Ave., Wheaton, Ill. 60187. (W) Scripture Press pass-along paper for older high school and college-age young people. Profiles (up to 2000 words) of contemporary Christians who would be of interest to older teens and whose lives demonstrate that Christianity works. First-person "as told to" teen experiences with Christian impact. Photo features of Christian teens in action. Ficton with teen flavor showing that Christ is the answer to teen needs. If unacquainted, ask for "Tips to the Writer" packet. Pays up to 3¢ a word.

GOOD NEWS BROADCASTER (interdenominational), Box 82808, Lincoln, Neb. 68501. (M) Mainly for adults, but includes articles for ages 18-25. Wants true stories on salvation and how to live the Christian life. Should be 1500 words. Pays up to 3¢ per word.

HIS, 5206 Main St., Downers Grove, Ill. 60515. Devotional, biographical, missionary, expository, theological articles; Christian evidences, carefully documented; poetry; college how-to-do-it in witnessing, etc.; other items of interest to college and university students. Pays 1¢ per word prior to publication.

INSIGHT (Young Calvinist Federation), Box 7244, Grand Rapids, Mich. 49510. (M) Desires feature articles (moral, educational, cultural guidance) and fiction and poetry with a Christian emphasis meaningful to youth, ages 16-22. Length: up to 2500 words. Pays up to $30.

LIGHTED PATHWAY (Church of God), 922 Montgomery Ave., Cleveland, Tenn. 37311. (M) Articles, 500-700 words, inspirational, didactic, how-to; fiction, 1200 words. All material must be religious, slanted for youth. Pays ½¢ per word.

REACH (Warner Press), Anderson, Inc. 46011. (M) Wants short stories up to 2200 words. General articles on Christian personalities, guidance and how-to-do-it themes should run not more than 1000 words. Pays $7.50 per 1000 words minimum. Poetry, 20¢ per line or $2.50 minimum for fewer lines, by youth only.

SCIENCE & SCRIPTURE, P. O. Box 1672, Beaumont, Tex. 77704. Wants simply-expressed articles which correlate conservative Biblical theology with science. Articles on dinosaurs, geology, evolution, space flight, etc. Some articles are paid for; others are not.

SENIOR HI CHALLENGE (Church of God Publ. House), 922 Montgomery Ave., Cleveland, Tenn. 37312. (W) Wants stories of young Christians in today's world, biographies, short inspirational fillers, camp experiences, mission stories, profiles of young people engaged in Christian work. Length: 400-1200 words. Pay ½¢ a word.

THE STUDENT (The Sunday School Board of the Southern Baptist Convention), 127 Ninth Ave., N., Nashville, Tenn. 37203. (M) Occasionally buys from free-lance writers. Short stories concerning typical campus situations, typical students, 1500-1800 words. Factual articles concerning campus morals, problems of students, etc., 1000-1500 words. Good poetry, usually free verse, slanted toward students. Devotional and inspirational materials. Activities of other campus student groups in article form, sometimes used with pictures, 500-800 words. Pays upon publication, 2½¢ per word for prose; 35¢ per line for poetry.

YOUTH ALIVE (official organ of the Assemblies of God), 1445 Boonville Ave., Springfield, Mo. 65802. (M) Uses photo features, photos, interviews, forums, biographical features, reports on outstanding Christian youth, how-to-do-it features, some fiction, satire, humor, allegory, anecdotes, poems, news, motivational articles, testimonies, personal experiences, cartoons. Interested in second rights and other reprints. Pays 1¢ a word on acceptance (unless on assignment). Extra payment for photos submitted with articles.

26
The Early Teens

(ages 13-17)

From the moroseness of the 13-year-old to the "independence" of the 15-year-old, this early teen group is one of the most challenging to write for. Here's a brief summary of the three ages: 13's are interested in things around them but close-mouthed, inclined to keep things to themselves, critical of parents, worriers, often think in terms of hypothetical problems, and abhor the "kid stuff" of 11 and 12-year-olds; 14's are more self-assured, openly love their families, express themselves vigorously in talk and laughter; 15's take a backward dip in that they become apathetic again, muse much, are belligerent toward parents who try to "keep them babies," but respond to discussions. These young teens are the group to win for the Lord, to channel into service for Jesus Christ. By age 16, teens have matured into "young adults." Although they still resent restraint, they appreciate the need for self-discipline. They're looking seriously for answers to life. The older teens aren't as easy to win for the Lord but they must have Him as the foundation of their lives.

ALIVE, P.O. Box 179, St. Louis, Mo. 63166. Uses articles about outstanding youth; activities and projects of youth and youth groups; peer and parental relationships. For 12-14-year-olds. Lengths are from 1200 to 1500 words; pays 2¢ per word on acceptance.

AWARE, (American Baptist Board of Educational Ministries), Valley Forge, Pa. 19481. (M) Ages 13-18. News about youth achievements, articles on social issues, youth problems. Photos preferred with articles. Fiction should be full of adventure or romance. Very little poetry. Articles, 800-1000 words; fiction, 1800-2000 words. Payment: 1 to 2¢ a word; photos, $5 to $7.50.

BRIGADE LEADER (Christian Service Brigade), Box 150, Wheaton, Ill. 60187. (Q) Program helps for leaders of local church Brigade units. Suggestions for games, crafts and projects. Wants stories and talks for presentation to boys by their leaders, 500-1200 words. Two age groups: Stockade, 8-11 years; Battalion, 12-18 years. Must be Christ-centered, Biblically-based, life-related, specifically-aimed and have fitting content. Payment is 1/3¢ per word.

CAMPUS LIFE, Youth for Christ, Intl., P.O. Box 419, Wheaton, Ill. 60187. (M) Wants practical material dealing with the problems of modern Christian teen-agers. No sermons. Articles must be constructive and show understanding of adolescent minds and problems. Wants fiction which deals with Christian young people at school and home. Articles, 1600 words or less; fiction may go slightly longer. Pays 1½¢ per word and up, depending on quality.

CATALYST, Box 179, St. Louis, Mo. 63166. Articles of religious or social nature aimed at intelligent, concerned youth. Uses very little fiction. Payment is 1½¢ per word and up.

CHRISTIAN ADVENTURER (Pentecostal Church of God of America), P.O. Box 850, Joplin, Mo. 64801. (W) Teen-age take-home paper with articles of interest to youth and fiction with Christian purpose. Pays on acceptance ¼¢ per word. Uses poetry.

CHRISTSTYLE, Concordia Pub. House, 3558 S. Jefferson Ave., St. Louis, Mo. 63118. Discussion courses for high school youth, target age 14-16. Includes some poetry, motivational essays, short-short stories, posters, etc. tied to quarterly themes. Payment $10 and up. Prospectus gives future themes and due dates.

CONQUEST, (Church of the Nazarene), 6401 The Paseo, Kansas City, Mo. 64131. (M) Short stories up to 2500 words. No serials. Articles preferably illustrated with good photos. No sermons or sermonettes. Slanted to high school level. Poetry maximum, 20 lines. Pays 1¢ per word and up; $3 per accompanying photo; minimum 10¢ per line for poetry.

ENCOUNTER, Box 2000, Marion, Ind. 46952. (W) Address submissions to Editor of Sunday School Magazines. For senior teens, ages 15-18. Special issues for all religious and national holidays. Submit special material 9 months in advance. No query required. Uses 1000-2500-word fiction with definite Christian emphasis and character building values, without being preachy. Setting, plot and action should be realistic. Accepts serials of 6-8 chapters. Feature articles, with photos, will be considered. Also limited amount of poems for teens, 4-16 lines. Pays 2¢ a word for prose, 25¢ a line for poetry.

HICALL, (Gospel Publishing House), 1445 Boonville Ave., Springfield, Mo. 65802. Fiction, 1200-1800 words, presenting realistic characters dealing with Christianity in action. Not preachy. Non-fiction, 750-1000 words, includes biography, nature, scientific or missionary material with a spiritual lesson. Brief, purposeful fillers, up to 300 words, with strong evangelical emphasis. All special day material should be sent

10 to 12 months in advance. Payment is ½¢ to 1¢ per word on acceptance.

HIGH (Harvest Publications and Gospel Light Publications), 1233 Central, Evanston, Ill. 60201. (W) Wants 500-1000-word teen-interest articles, preferably with photos, with definite evangelical angle; 1400-1500-word fiction. Pays 4¢ per word and up, month after acceptance; $2-$6 per photo. Query advisable. Complete packet of samples, suggestions and specifications for *High* and other take-home papers, 50¢.

MY DELIGHT, Union Gospel Press, Box 6059, Cleveland, Ohio 44101. (W) Uses real-life stories and fiction with evangelical Christian emphasis, from 925 to 1500 words in length. Short devotional articles of approx. 300 words. Pays 2¢ per word. A teen take-home paper.

REACHOUT, Light and Life Press, Winona Lake, Ind. 46590. (W) Wants good fiction, aimed at teens in grades 7-9, of 1800-2000 words. Serials should not be more than 8 chapters with each chapter about 1800 words. Uses biographical articles (the subjects should be deceased) and personality articles of 200-1000 words. Good quality photos enhance the salability of articles. Uses 4-16-line poetry. Payment is 2¢ a word for prose, 25¢ a line for poetry.

STRAIGHT, Standard Publishing, 8121 Hamilton Ave., Cincinnati, Ohio 45231. (W) Wants character-building fiction with appeal to teen-agers to correlate with International Bible-school lessons, if possible. Must be submitted at least six months in advance of publication date. Length of stories; 1500-1800 words. Articles about Christian athletes with photos. Length of articles; 750-1000 words. Payment is determined by length and quality.

TEEN POWER, 1825 College Ave., Wheaton, Ill. 60187. (W) Scripture Press take-home paper for 12-14-year olds. All material should in some way relate to Christian living. Uses 1000-1500-word teen experiences, profiles of youth and adults, photo stories of youth in action for the church and God. Fiction. Get acquainted with this market through "Tips to Writer" packet, free on request. Pays 3¢ a word.

TEENS TODAY, 6401 The Paseo, Kansas City, Mo. 64131. (W) Stories showing senior highs solving true-to-life situations through the application of Christian principles. Stories should portray definite Christian emphasis, but not be preachy. Setting, plot and action should be realistic. Write for free folder, "Suggestions to Contributors," for greater detail and denominational taboos of Church of the Nazarene. Article length: 800-1200 words; fiction to 2500 words. Pays 2¢ a word on acceptance.

WIND, Box 2000, Marion, Ind. 46952. *Wind* is the official paper of The Wesleyan Youth organization. Wants articles on careers, devotional, inspirational, biographical, seasonal, sports, historical, poetic, humorous—anything youth related. Uses short stories. Pays ½¢ per word; payment for poetry varies.

YOUTH IN ACTION (Free Methodist Church), Winona Lake, Ind. 46590. (M) Official youth publication of the denomination. The style of writing should be appropriate for high school young people, focusing on the sophomore-junior level. Uses a variety of material, both fiction and nonfiction, cartoons, fillers, poetry by teen-agers. Fiction should be from 500 to 2000 words (preferred length 1000-1500 words); nonfiction, 250-2000 words. Payment is 1½¢ per word for prose, $5 each for photos.

27
The Transition Period

(ages 9-13)

This can be a difficult age. They've learned that adults are not always right. They want facts, although they enjoy a good exciting story. They want to do things with their hands. They firmly believe they're right—always. And they're intensely loyal. You must show them you know what you're talking about; then you can lead them. But don't talk down to them or scold, for they resent it.

ACCENT ON YOUTH, The United Methodist Pub. House, 201 Eighth Ave. S., Nashville, Tenn. 37203. (M) Articles, 800-1200 words, 3¢ a word and up. Short stories, 1500-2200 words, $75 and up. Photo features, cartoons, photographs (8 x 10 black and white; color transparencies). Teen activities. Self-guidance; health, personality, behavior, etiquette, etc. Faith and ethics. Especially slanted to junior high understanding and experience. Fine and popular arts. Public affairs and social issues, sciences and the natural world, biblical and theological issues.

ADVENTURE (Southern Baptist Convention), 127 Ninth Ave. N., Nashville, Tenn. 37234. (W) Wants illustrated articles, up to 650 words, on nature, travel, science, games, features, how-to. Wants stories, up to 900 words, for boys and girls 8-11-years-old. Stories of wholesome adventure or achievement rank high. A limited number of puzzles, quizzes, etc., are used. Poems of 4-24 lines. Pays 2½¢ per word on acceptance.

ADVENTURE (Harvest Publications and Gospel Light Publications), 1233 Central, Evanston, Ill. 60201. (W) Uses features on children's Christian service activities, true-life adventure and short stories, 1400-1500 words, for children in grades 4-6. Every item must convey an unmistakable but smoothly integrated spiritual idea. Pays 3¢ and up, month after acceptance. Query advisable. Packet of samples, suggestions and specifications for *Adventure* and other take-home papers, 50¢.

CLIMB (Publication Board of the Church of God), Box 2499, Anderson, Ind. 46011. (W) Aimed for the 10-year-old reader, it wants fiction and nonfiction that deals with Christian living and example. Fiction stories, 800 to 1200 words, should challenge and guide readers in the meaning of living a winsome, Christian life. Nonfiction should be shorter to provide space for photographs—about 950 words. Payment is on acceptance at the rate of $7.50 per 1000 words. Poetry is 20¢ per line or $2 per poem.

COUNSELOR, 1825 College Ave., Wheaton, Ill 60187. (W) Scripture Press take-home paper for children 9-11. Specializes in true stories that demonstrate the thrill of walking with Christ. Wants interesting true stories with good photos. Length of stories, 600-1200 words. Query first. Free "Tips to Writer" packet gives more information. Pays 3¢ a word.

128

DISCOVERY, Light and Life Press, Winona Lake, Ind. 46590. (W) Needs stories of 1800-2000 words; articles, 200-1000 words, with pictures or sketches; short poetry. Special needs are seasonal materials, eight months in advance. Pays 2¢ per word, shortly after acceptance.

FIVE/SIX, 201 Eighth Ave., S., Nashville, Tenn. 37203. (W) Church history and biblical stories, 1250 words; modern-day stories, 1250 words; science and nature articles, 500 words; travel stories or stories of other countries, 500 words; puzzles, riddles, cartoons, how-to-do-it crafts. Photographs in b/w or color transparencies are used. Will report on mss. within three months. For 10- and 11-year-olds. Payment on acceptance. Minimum 3¢ per word plus additional payment for art work or photos. Poetry, $1 per line. Buys all rights; permission is given for book rights.

THE FRIEND, 50 East North Temple, Salt Lake City, Utah 84150. Short stories and serials for boys and girls up to 12 years of age. All stories must have a high motive, plot and action; must be wholesome and optimistic. Character-building stories preferred. Holiday stories good. No moralizing. Stories about children in other countries good. About 1000 words. Stories for younger children should not exceed 500 words. Short articles of current subjects, science, nature, pets, things to make or do are also acceptable. Pays on acceptance at 3¢ a word and up; verse 25¢ a line and up.

THE GOOD DEEDER, Your Story Hour, Berrien Springs, Mich. 49103. Character-building stories for boys and girls; target age is 10-14. Needs seasonal material, temperance material. Uses three lengths, about 750, 1000, 1500. Buys one-time rights; likes second rights material. Writers may send tear sheets. Pays 1¢ a word.

HIGHLIGHTS FOR CHILDREN, Honesdale, Pa. 18431. (M except July, Sept.) For children 3-12 years, this undenominational publication wants stories which the preschool child will listen to eagerly and the older child will also enjoy reading. Avoid references to crime or violence. Should be moral but not necessarily religious; never Sunday-schoolish. Also wants novel things to make and do. Pays 5¢ to 15¢ per word for stories on acceptance. Stocked with verse.

JET CADET, Standard Publishing, 8121 Hamilton Ave., Cincinnati, Ohio 45231. (W) Wants action-packed short stories of 900-1200 words; 500-800 word short articles; also handicraft ideas and hobby articles. Bible puzzles only. Pays up to 1½¢ per word.

JUNIOR DISCOVERIES (Church of the Nazarene), 6401 The Paseo, Kansas City, Mo. 64131. (W) Fiction 1200 words, serials of 3 or 4 parts, 5000 words. Feature articles, 500-750 words. Photos or other illustrative material welcome. Photos should be glossy, 5 x 7 or 8 x 10. Pays $20 per 1000 words on acceptance; $1-$10 for photos; poetry, 4-16 lines, 25¢ per line and up.

JUNIOR LIFE (Pentecostal Church of God of America), P.O. Box 850, Joplin, Mo. 64801. (W) Sunday school take-home paper for ages 9-11. Uses mostly fiction and fillers. Pays on acceptance, ¼¢ per word. Uses poetry.

JUNIOR TRAILS, Gospel Publishing House, 1445 Boonville Ave., Springfield, Mo. 65802. (W) Fiction, from 1500-1800 words, presenting Christianity in action. Biography, missionary material using fiction technique. Historical, scientific or nature material with a spiritual lesson, 500-1000 words. Fillers, up to 200 words, containing an anecdote and with strong evangelical slant. Puzzles and quiz material based on the Bible are used. Special day material should be sent 10 to 12 months in advance. Pays upon acceptance from ½¢ to 1¢ per word.

MY DEVOTIONS (Lutheran: Missouri Synod), Concordia Pub. House, 3558 S. Jefferson Ave., St. Louis, Mo. 63118. (M) Monthly booklet of devotional reading for ages 8 to 13.

Devotions should be evangelical, based on the Gospel and related to life. Average length: 300 words. Payment is $7.50 per devotion. Few free-lance mss. accepted. Must enclose self-addressed stamped envelope.

MY PLEASURE, Union Gospel Press, Box 6059, Cleveland, Ohio 44101. (W) True-life stories or fiction from 750 to 1400 words with Christian emphasis. Also short devotional articles of approximately 275 words, quizzes and puzzles. Pays 2¢ per word. It is a Junior take-home paper.

ON THE LINE (Mennonite), 616 Walnut Ave., Scottdale, Pa. 15683. (W) Needs wholesome stories for the modern child, 1000-1200 words, encouraging Christian attitudes toward himself and others and the situations in which he finds himself. Serials to five parts. Needs articles, 800-1200 words, designed to increase the child's interest in Christianity; his understanding of the Bible; his identification with church; nature and hobbies. Pays about 1½¢ per word (¾¢ per word for second rights mss). Also uses verse, 4-16 lines; often semihumorous with unexpected twist; puzzles and quizzes; photos with outstanding visual appeal, mostly of animals or children (ages 9-14). "When You Write" brochure and sample copies free on request.

PARTNERS, Christian Light Publications, Inc., P.O. Box 833, Harrisonburg, Va. 22801. Uses articles, up to 400 words; stories, 800-1600 words; poems and songs. For ages 9-14. All material should be Bible-centered, speaking to a child's spiritual needs. A writer's guide is available by writing. Send all mss. to Evelyn B. Bear, Editor, P.O. Box 3116, Elida, Ohio 45807.

THE YOUNG CRUSADER (WCTU), 1730 Chicago Ave., Evanston, Ill. 60201. (M) Stories under 850 words with total abstinence, junior science or nature theme and slanted to 6-12-year-old readers. Pays ½¢ per word on acceptance.

WHENEVER WHATEVER, American Baptist Board of Ed. & Publ., Valley Forge, Pa. 19481. (M) For boys and girls, grades 5 and 6. Needs stories to 1500 words; articles, 800-1000 words, on all subjects; biographies; poetry; puzzles, riddles. Needs seasonal emphasis. Pays 1 to 2¢ a word for stories and articles, 25¢ a line for poetry.

28
The Small Fry

(under age 9)

There are two distinct groups under this category. You'll notice that these publications are often for only one of the two groups—3 to 5-year-olds or 6 to 8-year-olds. If there's only one publication, usually it's slanted to the older group. Pre-school children love movement, rhythm, familiar things like home, pets, daily activities. They don't notice detail and time means little or nothing to them. Curious and inquisitive, they think in concrete pictures, rather than abstractions. The 6 to 8-year-old period is the "up and at 'em" time. They're learning to read, they're curious about the world around them, imaginative. Words are fascinating. Boys and girls often play separately now. Writing for these pre-Juniors can be fascinating—if you're fascinated by everything around you. There's still wonder here and simplicity. It's a good time to lead them into making a definite commitment of their lives to Christ.

4 & 5 STORY PAPER, Standard Publishing, 8121, Hamilton Ave., Cincinnati, Ohio 45231. (W) Church-related paper for 4 and 5-year-olds. Character-building stories to be read to children. These stories should be within the everyday experience of the child. Can use some seasonal stories, finger plays and rhymes (Bible characters, God's creations, Christian attitudes) and easy-to-do crafts. Payment shortly after acceptance; up to 1½¢ a word for stories; payment for other materials determined upon quality.

HAPPY TIMES, Concordia Pub. House, 3558 S. Jefferson Ave., St. Louis, Mo. 63118. (M) Wants material that strengthens and supports Christian home training by providing home activity suggestions, stories with Christian themes, poems. There is a pre-primary picture story. Buys all rights. Pays $3 to $7.50 per double-spaced page on publication.

MORE (Southern Baptist Convention), 127 Ninth Ave. N., Nashville, Tenn. 37234. (W) Wants stories and articles up to 600 words for boys and girls 6 and 7-years-old (1st and 2nd graders). Uses brief, illustrated articles of the how-to type, games, features, nature articles. Pays 2½¢ per word on acceptance.

NURSERY DAYS (Graded Press), 201 Eighth Ave. S., Nashville, Tenn. 37202. Methodist church-related story paper for nursery children, approx. 2 and 3-years-old. Stories up to 300 words; poems, prayers should be approx. 4 to 8 lines. Each mss. should be submitted typewritten on a separate sheet of paper. Buys all rights except in rare instances. Payment scale is basically as follows: stories, 4¢ a word; poems, $1 a line.

OUR LITTLE FRIEND, Pacific Press Pub. Assn., 1350 Villa St., Mountain View, Calif. 94040. (W) This is for children 2 to 6-years-old. They use stories, some poetry, puzzles, short filler material and special features. Story length is 600 to 1000 words. Small black-and-white pictures submitted with a manuscript to illustrate a story or poem increase the chance of sale. Payment is 1¢ a word for prose and 10¢ a line for poetry. Payment for photos is from 50¢ up.

PRIMARY TREASURE, Pacific Press Pub. Assn., 1350 Villa St., Mountain View, Calif. 94040. (W) Slanted for children 7 to 9 years. They use stories, some poetry, puzzles, short filler material and special features. Story length is 500 to 1500 words. Small black and white photos submitted with a manuscript to illustrate a story or poem increase the chance of sale. Payment is 1¢ a word for prose and 10¢ a line for poetry. Payment for photos is from 50¢ up.

ROADRUNNER, American Baptist Board of Ed. & Publ., Valley Forge, Pa. 19481. (W) For boys and girls, grades 1 and 2. Wants puzzles, dot-to-dot pictures, simple photographic essays, stories (no longer than 500 words), articles on all subjects (200-300 words), good poetry. Seasonal emphasis needed. Pays 1 to 2¢ a word, 25¢ a line for poetry.

STORY FRIENDS, Mennonite Publ. House, Scottdale, Pa. 15683. (W) Stories from everyday experiences at home, school and church; stories that answer children's questions about God, Jesus and the Bible and prayer; that give patterns of forgiveness, honesty and trust; that suggest experiences in giving; nature stories, stories for Christian holidays. Characters should come alive as real people. The above themes should be used without moralizing. 400-900 words. Payment upon acceptance, up to 1½¢ per word.

STORY MATES, Christian Light Publications, Inc., P.O. Box 833, Harrisonburg, Va. 22801. (W) Uses stories, songs, poems, craft ideas, puzzles for children 4-8. Story length is 400-800 words. All material should be Bible-centered, speaking to a child's spiritual needs; a writer's guide is available by writing. Send all manuscripts to Evelyn B. Bear, Editor, P.O. Box 3116, Elida, Ohio 45807.

WEEKLY BIBLE READER, Standard Publishing, 8121 Hamilton Ave., Cincinnati, Ohio 45231. (W) Needs stories of 250 to 300 words—stories that teach without preaching, stories for children, riddles, things to make or do. Materials should be aimed at 6 and 7-year-olds. Will buy simple cartoons that have nothing to be read. Will consider glossy photos—animals, nature study, children of the world. Pays $5 to $10 for stories, $1 to $5 for poems, puzzles, etc., up to $10 for photos.

WONDER TIME (Nazarene), 6401 The Paseo, Kansas City, Mo. 64131. (W) For children 6 to 8 years of age. Accepts stories and articles 200-750 words; also poems, 4-16 lines. Pays $20 for 1000 words and up; 12½¢ per line and up for poems.

29
Photographs

BRYSON, FRANKLIN, PHOTOGRAPHER, P.O. Box 1909, Pensacola, Fla. 32502. Prices are normally ASMP rates, but each assignment would be handled as to the amount of work, material and time it takes. Handles color or B&W, single pictures or picture stories, straight photographs or interpretive as the writer desires.

EUROPEAN ART COLOR SLIDES, Peter Adelberg, Inc. 120 W. 70th St., New York, N.Y. 10023. 4,500 items: Original color transparencies featuring an outstanding collection of transparencies to illustrate the great ideas found in religion. Paintings, frescoes, mosaics, stained glass windows, illuminated manuscripts, sculpture, architecture, churches, views, tapestries, etc. From prehistoric to contemporary art. All photographed ON THE SPOT in Europe, Egypt, Mexico, Yucatan, Guatemala. Print and reproduction fees charges. Price upon request. Detailed information available as to subject, artist and his work. Set of catalogues $1.25.

FREELANCE PHOTOGRAPHERS GUILD, INC., 110 W. 32nd St., New York, N.Y. 10001. "World's largest agency for color photographs." One million color transparencies, three million B&W photos. Every conceivable subject available for advertising, printing and publishing. Price depends on ultimate use. Let us help you with your picture needs.

HACKETT, G.D., STUDIO, 130 West 57th Street, New York, N.Y. 10019. Has great variety of photo subjects: pictorials, press-portraits of famous people in politics and arts, documentaries showing war, slums, degradation. Send in subject of book and receive quote on photos. 20 years' experience in serving the book industry. Authors' portraits. Press and publicity photos. 10,000 items: B&W original and copy photos, color transparencies, slides, clippings, post cards, old prints, art reproductions. Subjects include art, music, celebrities, New York, France, Hungary, Austria, World War II, concentration camps, Jewish persecution, American Indians. Open to qualified researchers for editorial and advertising use. Reproduction fee charged.

30
Feature Syndicate

MID-CONTINENT FEATURE SYNDICATE, Box 1662, Pittsburgh, Pa. 15230. (D) This syndicate provides some 600 small and medium-sized daily newspapers on the American continent with features such as columns (books, women's, business, human interest, comics and panels) in addition to a wide range of photo features, book digests, etc. Payment upon acceptance at the usual rate for feature materials.

31
Book Publishers

AUGSBURG PUBLISHING HOUSE, 426 S. 5th St., Minneapolis, Minn. 55415. Types of books wanted. Non-fiction: they publish a variety of books for children, teen-agers, laymen, ministers, church school teachers and scholars. Subject areas include theology, Bible study, church history, biography, sermons, teaching aids, devotionals, social issues, personal problems and church life. Fiction: they publish novels, drama and poetry for children and adults. These mss. should reflect the Christian faith but not be overly preachy or dogmatic. They look for mss. that reflect the historic biblical tradition, but show an awareness of the contemporary world and that are written in a fresh, interesting style.

BAKER BOOK HOUSE, 1019 Wealthy St. S.E., Grand Rapids, Mich. 49506. They want nonfiction manuscripts from 30,000 to 60,000 words.

CELESTIAL PRESS, 868 Grant Ave., Novato, Calif. 94947. They publish both fiction and nonfiction. They like at least 50,000 words.

CREATION HOUSE, 499 Gundersen Drive, Carol Stream, Ill. 60187. Their emphasis is on Christian biography, the charismatic movement, and Christianity and culture.

CUSTOMBOOK, INC., 30 Ruta Court, So. Hackensack, N.J. 07606. They specialize in publishing stories about church histories, community histories and stories published in connection with special events in the congregation. The text usually is combined with attractive photos in color and black and white so that the final result is similar to magazine format.

DIMENSION BOOKS, P.O. Box 811, Denville, N.J. 07834. They publish nonfiction books of about 25,000 words by established writers only.

DOUBLEDAY & COMPANY, INC., 277 Park Ave., New York, N.Y. 10017. They want both fiction and nonfiction at 50,000 words plus.

FLEMING H. REVELL COMPANY, Old Tappan, N.J. 07675. They want nonfiction at about 30,000 words.

FORTRESS PRESS, 2900 Queen Lane, Philadelphia, Pa. 19129. Wants only nonfiction manuscripts.

FOUNTAINHEAD PUBLISHERS, INC., 475 Fifth Ave., New York, N.Y. 10017. Wants nonfiction at about 75,000 words. An author must request permission to send in a mss. A complete biography about the author: age, education, when ordained, where, if spiritual leader of congregation, if published previously, etc.

FREEMAN PUBLISHING COMPANY LIMITED, Saskatoon, Sask., Can. S7K 3R8. Uses nonfiction of theology, philosophy, inspirational from 30,000 to 50,000 words. Must be orientated to orthodox Christian theology, biblically based, non-sectarian.

GRIFFIN HOUSE, 455 King St. W., Toronto 135, Ont., Can. Wants non-fiction manuscripts.

HARPER & ROW, 10 E. 53 St., New York, N.Y. 10022.

A. J. HOLMAN COMPANY (Division of J. B. Lippincott Company), East Washington Square, Philadelphia, Pa. 19105. Wants both nonfiction and fiction of about 30,000 words.

INTER-VARSITY PRESS, Box F, Downers Grove, Ill. 60515. Wants books which present biblical Christianity to an intelligent Christian or non-Christian audience; these books may range from expositions of Scripture, presentations of theological scholarships, analyses of society and culture from a biblical perspective and help in living the Christian life for Christians of all spiritual ages.

JOHN KNOX PRESS, Box 1176, Richmond, Va. 23209. Rarely buys fiction. Types of religious books wanted: books dealing with prayer and personal faith; family and interpersonal relationships; inspirations; biblical and theological scholarship and the relation of religion to social, cultural, ethical or aesthetic concerns. It would be helpful if the author's covering letter includes a brief description of the book's potential market and its uniqueness in the field.

JUDSON PRESS, Valley Forge, Pa. 19481. Buys nonfiction—inspirational, personal experience—of about 45,000 words.

LIBRA PUBLISHERS, INC., P.O. Box 165, 391 Willets Rd., Roslyn Heights, L.I., New York 11577. Wants both fiction and nonfiction with a minimum of 20,000 words.

MOODY PRESS, 820 N. LaSalle St., Chicago, Ill. 60610. They are a general publisher, so both fiction and nonfiction should contain a distinctly Christian message. For fiction, they prefer the complete manuscript. For non-fiction, particularly textbook-level material, they prefer a query containing the outline and sample chapters.

SHEED & WARD, INC., 64 University Pl., New York, N.Y. 10003. Wants nonfiction manuscripts.

STANDARD PUBLISHING, 8121 Hamilton Ave., Cincinnati, Ohio 45231. Publish children's picture story books, 16 or 24 pages, for children, 3 to 8. Stories should be Bible-based or contain definite Christian teaching. Payment varies, depending on quality and length. Also wants pocketbook, 96 pages, for pre-teens, teens and adults. Christian fiction, current teen problems and interests, devotional books. Payment varies, depending on quality and length.

WORD BOOKS, Box 1790, Waco, Tex. 76703. Wants nonfiction manuscripts of about 60,000 words.

ZONDERVAN, Grand Rapids, Michigan 49506.

32
Roman Catholic Book Publishers

ABBEY PRESS, St. Meinrad, Ind., 47577. Wants nonfiction of about 40,000 words.

OUR SUNDAY VISITOR, INC., Noll Plaza, Huntington, Ind. 46750. Accepts both nonfiction and textbooks on basic Roman Catholic religious topics. Texts on grade school, high school and adult education levels. From 50,000 to 100,000 words.

THE CATHOLIC UNIVERSITY OF AMERICA PRESS, INC., 620 Michigan Ave. N.E., Washington, D.C. 20017. Wants works of original scholarship in Catholic theology from 100,000 to 120,000 words.

ALBA HOUSE (A division of the Society of St. Paul), 2187 Victory Blvd., Staten Island, New York 10314. Wants nonfiction of about 55,000 words.

PFLAUM/STANDARD, 38 W. 5th St., Dayton, Ohio 45402. Their market is the Catholic school and adult discussion club market. Accept mss. from 20,000 to 35,000 that are nonfiction.

FRANCISCAN HERALD PRESS, 1434 W. 51st St., Chicago, Ill. 60609. Want books having to do with any aspect of Franciscanism, history, spirituality, literature. Also books on general Christian spirituality, history and life. Send letter of inquiry first before sending mss. Also be prepared to send chapter heads and sample chapter. Length: 25,000 to 30,000 words.

FIDES PUBLISHERS, INC., Box F, Notre Dame, Ind. 46556. Theological, scriptural, devotional and liturgical books in the high-popular level; religious education and related field, such as early childhood and value education. From 30,000 to 70,000 words.

Part Nine
Writers' Conferences

33
Writers' Conferences

CAPE CODE WRITERS CONFERENCE, Craigville Conference Center, Craigville (Cape Cod), Mass. 02636. In August. Courses for fiction, nonfiction, poetry and juvenile writing each day. Noted authors address the members each evening.

CHRISTIAN WRITERS INSTITUTE CONFERENCE AND WORKSHOP, Gundersen Dr. and Schmale Rd., Wheaton, Ill. 60187. This annual four-day conference usually is held the first week of June.

CONFERENCE ON WRITING AND LITERATURE, Wheaton College, English Department, Wheaton, Ill. 60187. This is an annual conference, usually held in October.

DECISION MAGAZINE SCHOOL OF CHRISTIAN WRITING, 1300 Harmon Pl., Minneapolis, Minn. 55403. An annual three-day summer conference.

MILDRED I. REID WRITERS' COLONY, Penacook Rd., Contoocook, N.H. 03229. Yearly from June 15 - Spetember 1. Tuition $60 to $70 weekly. Students may come for any length of time—one day to three months. Tuition includes breakfast, lunch, two private lessons each week, two roundtable classes each week. Some students may work for their tuition.

RHINELANDER SCHOOL OF ARTS, University of Wisconsin, 216 Agricultural Hall, Madison, Wis. 53706. For 10 days, usually the last of July, held in Rhinelander.

Part Ten
Writers' Clubs

34
Writers' Clubs

ASSOCIATED BUSINESS WRITERS OF AMERICA, Inc., P. O. Box 135, Monmouth Junction, N.J. 08852. Members are published free-lance writers, experienced in business journalism which covers advertising copy, public relations, ghost writing, books, reports, instruction manuals, etc. as well as business and technical magazines. ABWA publishes an annual directory profiling writers who are pre-checked with editors to determine ability and dependability. Each is listed geographically, giving phone, area covered, photo skill, special industry knowledge (latter indexed at back) and alphabetically. Directory price is $3. List of members geographically arranged is free. Regular monthly bulletin goes to members; pages are open to editors who desire special needs published for ABWA writers. Dues are $30 per year, payable semi-annually. ABWA is a professional organization of great value to writers who qualify for membership.

THE AUTHORS LEAGUE OF AMERICA, INC., 234 W. 44th St., New York, N.Y. 10036. A Nat'l membership corp., to promote the professional interests of authors and dramatists, procure satisfactory copyright legislation and treaties, guard freedom of expression and support fair tax treatment for writers. The Authors Guild, Inc. (Tel. 212-695-4145). The Dramatist Guild, Inc. (Tel: 212-563-2233).

CANADIAN AUTHORS ASSOCIATION, Yorkville Public Library, 22 Yorkville Ave., Toronto 5, Ont., Canada is the one national organization in Canada for writers. Its membership of close to 1000 is composed of writers of books, short stories, dramas, feature articles and poetry; and of others with a sincere interest in Canadian literature. It has no bias of politics, creed, race or color. National fees are $15 a year.

CHRISTIAN WRITERS' LEAGUE OF AMERICA, 4211 Olds Rd., Oxnard, Calif. 93030. This meets once a month for inspiration, information and inter-action on Christian writing. Interdenominational. Open to beginners as well as professionals. Welcome new branches throughout the country.

INDIANAPOLIS STORY-A-MONTH CLUB, 4186 Broadway, Indianapolis, Ind. Devoted to helping its members write salable prose. Monthly meetings at Broadway Branch Library. Writers and potential writers welcome.

NATIONAL ASSOCIATION OF GAGWRITERS, a division of the Humor Societies of America, sponsors Comedy Workshops of America in cities across the nation conducted by members of the Humor Exchange Network who are both gagwriters, comedians and cartoonist. In New York City, the Gagwriters-Comedy Workshop serves as a humor laboratory for testing talents and techniques, holding meetings two nights a week for two hours each night, featuring analysis of material and showcasings of both comedy writers and performers. Membership dues vary depending on needs of members, varying from $10 a year for students in high schools and colleges, to $25 a year for gagwriters who need greater services. Emphasis is on Income Production and Comedy Development spotlighting Future Funny Men & Women of America. Contact is George Q. Lewis, Director of the Humor Societies of America, 74 Pullman Ave., Elberon, N.J. 07740. Tel: 201-229-9472.

THE NATIONAL WRITERS CLUB, 1365 Logan St., Denver, Colo. 80203, was founded in 1937 by David Raffelock. It serves free-lance writers throughout North America by making available to them information, advice and help in all matters relating to writing for various markets. The club mentors all services offered to writers and reports on those that are either competent and reliable or those that prey on writers. NWC maintains continuing products to improve writer-editor relations by informing writers of professional requirements and standards. The club intercedes on behalf of members when editors fail to report on manuscripts or to pay for published material. An annual meeting is held in Denver during the winter months and a national workshop is conducted late in the spring. Regular meetings are held only by the several chapters of the organization. There are two classes of membership: associate for which the annual fee is $15 and full or professional for which the annual fee is $20. An outline of the club's services and a membership application form may be obtained by writing the secretary.

NEBRASKA WRITERS GUILD, 4865 Wirt St., Omaha, Neb. 68104. Meets twice a year, May and October in different parts of the state. A bulletin is published annually listing names and addresses of all members and brief accounts of the sales made by members, books published and current writing activities. To be eligible, applicants must have sold something they have written. Dues $5 annually.

OREGON CHRISTIAN WRITER'S ASSN., Multnomah School of the Bible, Portland, Ore.

RHODE ISLAND WRITERS' GUILD, 139 Colfax St., Providence, R.I. 02905. Active Associate, Shut-In, Junior memberships available, various dues. Members meet others who are interested in similar types of writing, such as hymns, fiction, nonfiction, poetry, etc. Referral services are available for help in technical aspects of publishing, promotion and personal attention.

WRITERS' CLUB OF WHITTIER, INC., 11036 E. Lorene St., Whittier, Calif. 90601. Meets in separate workshops—fiction, nonfiction, juvenile, poetry and drama-TV—once or twice monthly at the Whittier Recreational Center solely to read and criticize each other's mss. Annual dues $5 which entitles a member to attend all workshops for which he can qualify. Qualification for membership is publication in the field for which applicant applies, or submission of several mss. considered acceptable by a reading committee.